Power Moves

Power Moves

How Women Can Pivot, Reboot, and Build a Career of Purpose

Lauren McGoodwin

HARPER
BUSINESS

An Imprint of HarperCollinsPublishers

FIRST EDITION

Designed by Bonni Leon-Berman
Graphics designed by Paige Gutierrez

Library of Congress Cataloging-in-Publication Data has been applied for.

ISBN 978-0-06-290919-0

20 21 22 23 24   LSC   10 9 8 7 6 5 4 3 2 1

To my younger self, who was a terrible reader
but is now a published author.
You're capable of more than you know.

To my dad, for being a #girldad and always answering
my call when "I have an idea . . ."

To the Career Contessa team, community, and mentors,
who have inspired and impacted my work.

Contents

Introduction

Let's talk about self-improvement. As a culture, we're a bit obsessed with this concept because we've been programmed to believe that discomfort should be avoided, and that any uncomfortable feelings we experience should be mitigated immediately. I'm not talking about physical discomfort (by all means, please see the doctor)—I'm talking about the mental and emotional discomfort we all experience as we age.

We've learned that upward movement is "good" and sideways, backward, and any direction in between is "bad." These unrealistic expectations feed personal inflexibility because we're hardwired to believe that our next best move is always "up," and if it doesn't go that way, it's time to try a DIY human improvement project because if you can fix that "thing" that is wrong with you, then the rest will fall into place.

I'm *not* anti–self-improvement. I'm anti–self-improvement approaches where you never really get past improving to evolve and take action based on newfound awareness.

Rather than looking inward and focusing on ourselves, our popular approach to improvement is based on looking ahead and glancing around at others. It's based on doing more of what we're already doing and tightly editing the well-laid plan we've already set.

But have you ever noticed that when you reframe your expectations and attitude, and have trust in yourself to take action—especially when you are uncomfortable and lack direction—you start to see the solution?

These actions ultimately lead to making more progress, experiencing more moments of success on your terms, and enjoying the comforts of higher self-worth. You're not just improving, you're evolving. Success becomes about the practice that you're developing, not chasing the expectations.

Expectations become the delusional friends who keep your brain on a constant loop at night and make you believe that if you're not getting what you want it's because you're not trying hard enough, and this mind-set teaches you to attach your self-worth to unattainable definitions of success.

I totally get it. It was a series of events that challenged my own expectations around my career and led me here to writing this book, which is why expectations are a perfect place for us to start.

I've been a planner for as long as I can remember. You know the type, right? As a teenager, I craved the start of a new school year so I could plan for my future. In high school I was laser-focused on college applications, and in college I would meticulously plan out each week in my agenda to ensure I never missed an opportunity to advance. After college, however, my "perfect plan" was all but annihilated.

I graduated from the University of Oregon in 2009 during one of the worst recessions in modern history, with a degree in education, zero job prospects, and one hell of an expectation hangover. I had been the university career center's poster child. I networked like crazy, attended every career fair, and, of course, made a list that would outline my plan for landing a great career. Said "great career" would get me inside engaging and well-paying work. Before long, I'd be on the cover of the alumni magazine.

Yeah, it didn't quite go like that.

Eight months after graduation, after a few temporary jobs and a roommate named Mom, I moved to Los Angeles, hopeful for what a new city might have in store for me. I interviewed at more than fifteen companies for roles ranging from nonprofit development to public relations. I actually misspelled the word *experience* on my résumé, which a lovely interviewer at a PR agency circled in red for me over and over again. Luckily for both of us, that interview didn't last long.

My final interview during this never-ending tour de jobs was for an administrative assistant role at the dental school of a major university. While I wasn't thrilled about the role, it was 2010, and I was grateful just to have an opportunity to work when it seemed like everyone was desperate for a full-time job. But my confidence, optimism, and aspirations suffered from the experience.

About a year in, I hit my breaking point. My assignment for the day was to feed sheets of paper into the printer, one by one. All day. What was I doing here? What were all my prior hard work and planning really for? I was trapped and unsure of how I would ever escape.

I was in the midst of an ambition trap. My desire—and, let's face it, a feeling of entitlement—to have something bigger and better for my career had actually led me off course. I had been focused solely on what should happen, or at least what I *thought* should happen, and accumulating "trophies" to prove my progress. It felt like the career success train had left the station without me, even though I had a first-class ticket. And it got worse because there were no directions on what to do next.

I admit, I'm a millennial through and through. I was raised to believe that women can do it all. I watched my female role models on TV become doctors, lawyers, and businesswomen. I imagined myself partaking in enviable brunches discussing sex and the city with my girlfriends after sprinting through the airport in my stylish pantsuit. I attended college, embraced my independence, and had lofty (but vague) career goals that would make me "the successful one" at any cocktail party.

For all my ambition, saying yes, and leaning in, my debut into the working world wasn't even in the same zip code as my expectations. And in hindsight, I see that my expectations were largely built on definitions of success written by others and made visually appealing by TV, magazines, movies, and later through Pinterest, Instagram, and even blogs. While my expectations *were* real, the portrayed success they advertised was *not* real.

For years while working at the dental school, I studied (okay, obsessed over) the LinkedIn profiles of my peers, discussed potential career paths with my parents, and became infatuated with figuring out my next career move. I was convinced that if I had that answer, if I could just zero in on the exact job and path I wanted, I would quickly be on my way to professional greatness. Of course, that's not how it works.

I can't recall the exact moment, but it gradually became clear that something had to change because all the "right" ways had led me to feeding paper into a printer. ONE. SHEET. AT. A. TIME. I dropped the "poor, pitiful me" attitude (it really wasn't my best look), forgave myself for not having it all figured out (or at least pretended to), and decided I had to change my approach. As easy as I make it sound, it wasn't.

In retrospect, this was the decision that helped me move my career *and* life forward in a new direction, and led me to begin understanding and implementing Power Moves—those unexpected, not-always-conventionally advisable actions and behaviors that make it possible to find fulfilling work you love, on your own terms. Since then, Power Moves have guided me through every difficult stage of my career. They've helped me think more holistically about my ambitions, my challenges, and what I *really* want out of life. Power Moves are not only a unique approach to your career; they're also the kinds of tailored-to-you decisions you make to ensure you're living authentically and staying true to yourself—not some idea of what you should be.

Changing my approach to my career started slowly. At work I volunteered for a random assignment that introduced me to the world of professional recruiting, which opened a door I hadn't even known to exist, which eventually helped me pivot to a job in recruitment at Hulu, just a budding tech start-up in those days, and the first job I had where my values and skills aligned with the company and role.

Getting that job didn't happen overnight (even though it can be frustrating, the endurance required to navigate a long and labyrinthine hiring process, and overcome the anxiety and self-doubt it often conjures, is its own kind of Power Move). It involved some near-religious moments of attitude adjustment. It forced me to confront failure. And it opened even more doors of what could be. But the best part—after landing that job, I started to make Power Moves. I started to pursue a career on my terms. For the first time, I felt like I had some control over the path I would take, whatever it might be.

After several years and a lot of lessons at Hulu, it was time for the next challenge—and a huge Power Move. Guided by my Hulu experience and my master's thesis in 2013 on millennial women and career resources (yes, in the midst of all this I went back to school for my master's—in retrospect an even bigger Power Move than I'd realized at the time), I was inspired to launch Career Contessa, an online media platform and resource dedicated to providing women the very same career help I had needed. I left a job I loved and jumped headfirst into the world of entrepreneur-ship to help women build successful and fulfilling careers, on their terms. It was equally exhilarating and terrifying.

Warning: starting a company is full of discomfort, risk, and shattered expectations. And that's on a good day! It's an ongoing test of how well you can multitask and prioritize. It requires un-wavering confidence yet inspires constant fear. But no matter how challenging, building Career Contessa has been the most reward-ing endeavor and, so far, the greatest privilege of my life. Through it, I've spoken to thousands of women—as a coach, doing inter-views, leading webinars, at in-person events, by email, in DMs, etc.—and there is one thing that unites us all. We are profoundly challenged trying to have the career we want, no matter how hard we work, no matter how many of the "right" boxes we check.

That's why I wanted to write this book.

I want to share what I've learned from my personal career jour-ney and the countless lessons—with the full range of outcomes—from so many women. This is a book about the practice of Power Moves and how you can make them a part of your life. It's about the power of progress and career fulfillment. It's about developing an approach to managing your career, on your terms.

I know what it feels like to be lost, to be caught in the speed cy-cle of "what ifs," to constantly review the to-do list in an attempt to take the next step. I know tough transitions. I know what it's like to fall victim to your own ambition trap and not embrace flex-ibility as your best professional asset.

Even if your job is not a dead end, you might still feel like you're stuck and don't know how to get out or make progress. Or maybe you actually found your dream job and thought you'd figured it all out but now you're ready for something new, lost on where to begin because you don't want to start all over again.

This career block you're up against? It's not your fault. It's the result of a mind-set that you may not realize you even have—one that this book is here to help you change. It's the result of having a bias against the unplanned at all times. It's the result of thinking that Power Moves are out of reach for you—even though they definitely are not. In fact, you've probably made one at some point and not even known it.

My biggest Power Move resulted in Career Contessa—a comprehensive, authentic career resource for women, sans intimidating, alienating, or condescending business jargon, or guilting or pressuring them into what they "should" be doing. It's a multiplatform career development business that helps millions of women each year solve their biggest career challenges and offers them a better way forward. Since 2013, Career Contessa has grown to include daily advice, online courses, a jobs database, a career coaching service, and a growing, vibrant staff and community that I'm proud of and inspired by every day. It's purposeful work that I love, and work I would never have found if I weren't willing to push back against the norm.

Pushing Back

What to do now? Well, first off, accept that you don't have to stay where you are—it's not unfair to want more even if you have plenty. You don't have to accept broken, or blocked, or derailed, or whatever name we give to careers that don't offer fulfillment. By changing the way you think about your career, you can rewrite your story. Acknowledging a mind-set that you may not realize you even have is a Power Move anyone can make—one that this book is here to help you make—on your way to having the career you want.

In this book, I'll talk about how we got here and the traps that we fall prey to. I'll talk about making Power Moves—the big or small, strategic and thoughtful actions and shifts in thinking that will help you get up and out of feeling stuck and into new and more rewarding phases of your career. I'll talk about how to be intentional, how to have flexible plans that work for who you are and what you want, and how the world may change around you. I'll give you resources to help you start thinking by doing. We're going to get messy before we get clear.

But before we get there, let's start shifting your thinking now. *Start by telling yourself that you are better than a rigid plan or the clear path you thought you were promised. Your life is complex and unique, and it evolves every day, not every year or every five years.* Start reciting this mantra out loud right this second. Repeat it again. It will help you cut yourself some slack. That is something you definitely deserve.

And, after reading this book? I want you to believe this: that you will know yourself, where you are, and what you want professionally well enough to rally, to find the courage to pursue the next big dream, to support yourself emotionally and financially, and, ultimately, to follow a career path that feels personal and is filled with purpose.

PART I

Does This Sound Familiar?

O n the surface, we live in a culture that shouts, "You can do anything!" Most of us have near-constant access to extensive, loving, and supportive networks (thanks to social media, texts, email, and more!) that reinforce this belief. What could be better?! We're bursting with confidence and seemingly unstoppable.

But it's not so simple. Because that mind-set comes with a major speed bump. While we approach the world with bold expectations and a clearly charted path to success, we quickly find the world doesn't always cooperate.

Most of us had (or will soon have!) the same disorienting experience. By the time we are firmly in our twenties, we realize the inverse was true—that our careers will pivot, veer, double back, and suddenly pitch forward until we find ourselves so far from our intended destination, we're practically on another continent. And to make matters worse, we all know this "American dream" we bought into is a lie, but we keep striving for it anyway.

So how exactly did we end up so far from our expectations? Understanding why we had those expectations, and the mind-set that still persists, is essential to learning how we'll guide our career moves in the future. Let's go back to the beginning.

CHAPTER 1

How Did We Get Here?

It all starts with millennials. Well, it actually all starts with generations of parents and their children; with decades-long attempts to overcome systemic sexism, racism, and economic inequality, to find work-life balance, to "have it all," and every other buzzy phrase you've heard and read in vintage career guides. But for our purposes—and the purposes of understanding just how you got to your current state of professional malaise and why it's increasingly hard to maintain your ambition—let's focus on millennials (with the caveat that even if you're not a millennial, anyone living and working right now has been and continues to be impacted by everything I'm about to explain).

According to most, the first millennial woman was born on January 1, 1982, and the last on December 31, 2000. We are the last to be born in the twentieth century and, since then, have become the most studied generation of all time.

But even with all this research, the findings about millennials (particularly around work and money) are often wildly contradictory, if not downright false. One school of thought says we're lazy and entitled people who live with our parents, can't manage money, and don't understand how work *works*. On the other side, we're considered fearless, authority-demolishing entrepreneurs who flout career conventions and demand flexibility while disrupting corporate paradigms and norms. Neither of these notions quite gets at the truth. And understanding the truth about millennials' professional lives is the key to understanding the seismic shift that's happened in work over the past fifteen years—not just to us, but to everyone.

For many millennials, planning for college started early in our high school years because competition for college acceptance had become fierce—the math was simple but problematic: there were more of us applying but the same number of spots to get in. Blame it on aspirational parents or the idea that a college degree can somehow guarantee a better life, but a study from the Pew Research Center found that there are more college-educated young adults now than ever before—in 2016 40 percent of millennials ages twenty-five to twenty-nine had a bachelor's degree (compare this to 2000, when 32 percent of Gen Xers were college educated, and 1985, when 26 percent of baby boomers received the same degrees). "The demand for higher education has risen dramatically since 1985," author and professor of economics Richard Vedder explained to *Business Insider* in 2018. With this demand came lowered chances of admission. Hence, the hustle.

The news was better for women, who were not only accepted to universities more frequently than men—making up 56 percent of all college admissions (a number that is rising)—but also crammed and outperformed our male counterparts once we got there.

Most of us graduated from college with outsize expectations. Many of us had no specific dreams, but instead attended college because our generation was "supposed to" or because we were born into the kind of privileged environment that just funneled us there, often without the benefit of time to think about what we even wanted to do with a degree once we got one (beyond just the nebulous concept of becoming "hirable").

We knew we'd have to work hard to achieve our dreams, but what we didn't anticipate was the powder keg the world was placing before us: a set of cultural, financial, and social shifts that would make it harder to succeed than we'd ever imagined—and when and if we did, the cost to our ambition, hope, and personal well-being would be higher than we'd ever thought possible. So, how exactly did all of this happen?

Family Matters

It's impossible to look at the millennial career trajectory without first understanding the unique way we were raised. Unlike generations before us, millennials grew up being the most important responsibility of our younger baby boomer and older Gen X parents, who (generally speaking) made it a priority to be extremely involved in our lives and to place more value on nurturing the family unit than their parents or grandparents had before them. This hyperattentiveness fueled a new focus on child safety and child protections, a movement that included new laws and regulations around how we ate and slept, what we drank, how we could ride in cars or on bikes or even walk down the street. It begot the popularity of babyproofing devices, BABY ON BOARD stickers, attachment and helicopter styles of parenting, and an overall "overprotection" ethos, the effects of which researchers are just beginning to unpack and understand today.

This new parenting paradigm, brought to you by the boomers and Gen Xers, included self-esteem classes, participation trophies, educational television, a variety of after-school activities to keep us well-rounded, and new metrics to raise the bar in education. And, not to be forgotten, we were all "special."

An expectation for our ultimate adult "success" led parents to organize their children's free time with activities to put them ahead of their peers. Because of this, we were rarely alone with our thoughts, and our free time was often not free but was instead overscheduled in an attempt to help us excel further and move faster.

One result of all this is we became a generation nearly incapable of operating without a well-formed structure. Millennials desire structure so we can gauge our performance (the focus on achievement also made us hyperaware of how we are doing when stacked against our peers—which is part of why, along with the omnipresence of social media, so many of us engage in "compare and despair," a phrase first coined by Dr. Alyssa Westring, a professor of management at DePaul University, but more on this later).

Another result of this type of parenting, of having our parents so involved in our lives, is that millennials have a deeply ingrained desire for feedback. So strong is our need for frequent feedback that without it we often get stuck and don't know what to do next. We depend on feedback and recognition to motivate and guide us to our next steps.

And, as if this feedback neediness wasn't enough to stress over, research shows that millennials are also always trying to do more and be better. Being a type-A perfectionist is the norm of this generation, rather than an outlier, as we are terrified that any mistake will drastically affect our future. Extreme ambition and drive are the outcome of the pressure we felt as children—we are a busy, purposeful group always looking to strive for more, but often without enough hours in a day to complete what we want. We are all the Energizer Bunny from our youths—we keep going and going and going . . . until we eventually flame out.

Ladies First

Adding to this pressure—and perhaps as a response to second-wave feminism or a desire to further advance the mission they began—baby boomer and Gen X moms were particularly active in pushing their millennial daughters to succeed. Our generation of women was specifically directed to "do it all." As Courtney E. Martin wrote in her book *Perfect Girls, Starving Daughters*, "we are a generation of young women who were told we could do anything and instead heard that we had to be everything."

We were held to high standards, but also held to the notion that we could have successful careers and picture-perfect family lives, and maintain our emotional and physical health while doing it—if only we were willing to put in the work. This messaging didn't only come from our mothers, of course. The myth of "having it all" was ingrained in us early by our parents and teachers, sure, but since then, entire forests have been cut down and turned into books that taught us to lean in, take a seat at the table, have confidence, own the room, do more, be better. The culmination of which is we have become human DIY projects, our social media feeds flashing motivation and inspiration constantly, encouraging the hustle, sending the absolute message that hard work will bring success as long as you invest in yourself.

And unlike previous generations of women, we grew up consuming media that illustrated an unrealistic picture of success, assured us that as long as we had the prerequisites (i.e., education, social skills, motivation, etc.) to be successful, It. Would. Happen. For.

Us. Although this message fed the need for structure and order that many millennials crave, it also built anxiety around measuring success in a world that doesn't give out trophies or actually care about graduation rankings.

This pressure to succeed has left an entire generation with a desire for direction, to retain minute-by-minute control over their lives and to strategize for the future—it also left us with new challenges to overcome. We submerge ourselves in plans, lists, and nonstop work; we need to know what's ahead of us, and we turn to the multitudes of online advice and life hacks, cultlike apps, and secret social media groups that capitalize on and enable our obsession for efficiency.

Thanks to technology and the internet (remember, millennials are the first generation of digital natives), we have become more adept at multitasking and scheduling, we pack our days with ambitious to-do lists and squeeze in extra appointments, we may even regularly pencil in self-care, but, if we're honest with ourselves, we know that, really, we are always on and always living in a crisis of expectations.

It's the Economy, Duh

For several years before and up until the fall of 2008, the financial picture for lots of millennials looked sunny. Many were raised in dual-income households and were surrounded by more wealth than their parents and previous generations. But in the fall of 2008, the financial collapse wiped out the investments, retirement plans, and income potential of many baby boomers and Gen Xers. While the economic crisis and subsequent recession most actively impacted the generations before us, that doesn't mean millennials were left unscathed. In fact, we are still learning just how much impact it had on our lives, in ways obvious and covert.

Debt Nation

Perhaps the most universally recognized financial characteristic of millennials (beyond overpaying for avocado toast) is the fact that many of us are struggling under the weight of crippling student loans. We're the most educated generation in US history, but the rise of tuition moved faster than our salaries, and our degrees came with higher expectations and higher stakes, including debt. The 2008 financial crisis—along with a complicated and delayed economic recovery—meant that many of us thought we had had no choice but to take on outsize loans to cover education costs in order to be on the path to career success.

In 2017, the average millennial American's student debt was around $50,000 (the country's total is $1.5 trillion, which is now higher than credit cards or car loans). The average student loan payment is $350 a month, payment that is around 8 to 10 percent of our incomes and more than the average US household spends on groceries. Proportionally, millennials, and particularly millennials of color, use more of their income to pay down student loan debt than anyone else. And the financial snapshot gets worse from there: when adjusted for inflation, our wages are, on average, lower than any have been since 1984.

Add this to ever-rising housing, health-care, and child-care costs, and the picture becomes even more bleak. Student debt is holding us back from doing what generations did before us: saving money for retirement, purchasing a home, investing, and generally feeling financially stable or safe.

In a 2017 *Forbes* article titled "The Impact of Student Loan Debt on Millennial Happiness," writer Sarah Landrum outlines precisely why this matters, explaining, "The size of our paychecks is, practically speaking, immaterial if we're not already on sound financial footing. In other words: Debt is a happiness killer. None of us can be truly happy if we're saddled with debt."

She goes on to say that "the specter of student loan debt nearly extinguishes the joy we associate with graduating from college in the first place." Landrum describes a "kind of 'tipping point' where the accrual of personal debt shifts from 'acceptable investment' to 'source of existential dread.'"

Mind the Pay Gap

Today, women attend college and receive degrees more than men, yes, but despite this educational advantage, we're still earning a hell of a lot less than our male counterparts, in virtually every industry. Although the Equal Pay Act was enacted in 1963, as I'm writing this in 2019, women are still only making 79 cents for every dollar earned by a man according to PayScale's The State of the Gender Pay Gap report.

The situation is even more dire for women of color. Black women earn 62 cents and Latinas earn 54 cents for every dollar paid to a white man.

These statistics hold almost universally true in the US, across industries and qualifications—women are paid less than men. And, shockingly, even education level doesn't significantly change the data. According to a 2018 analysis by Georgetown University's Center on Education and the Workforce, if you are female with a bachelor's degree you can expect to earn the salary of a man with an associate degree. (This holds true for every degree after it: If you're a woman with a master's degree, you'll get the equivalent of a man with a bachelor's. Get all the way to a doctorate? Expect to take home the same paycheck as your male colleague with a master's degree.) Men are also more likely to be promoted than women and with promotions come raises and, thus, the earnings gap gets bigger.

While we have made great strides in the past few decades for bringing awareness to the issue of wage gaps, there's still a long way to go until we achieve income equality—by some estimates, if things change at the pace they have since 1963, we'll reach earning parity by 2059, just as many of us will be ready to retire.

Jobs but No Job Security

This generation's financial crisis not only affected the housing and stock markets, it also deeply impacted the jobs in America—and not only for a few months, but for years that followed. The labor market would lose nearly nine million jobs by 2010, with some industries collapsing altogether and still more unable to recover completely even now, a decade later.

In her 2018 viral article "How Millennials Became the Burnout Generation," writer Anne Helen Peterson explains it this way:

> The crisis affected everyone in some way, but the way it affected millennials is foundational: It's always defined our experience of the job market. More experienced workers and the newly laid-off filled applicant pools for lower- and entry-level jobs once largely reserved for recent graduates. We couldn't find jobs, or could only find part-time jobs, jobs without benefits, or jobs that were actually multiple side hustles cobbled together into one job. As a result, we moved back home with our parents, we got roommates, we went back to school, we tried to make it work. We were problem solvers, after all—and taught that if we just worked harder, it would work out.

Even if you could/did find work when you left college, it still did not live up to the expectations of a sufficient middle-class income with benefits and long-term job security—the things you'd essentially been promised if you just did everything right. Which, as we know, you *did*.

The repercussions of this recession were myriad: the job market changed, the number of full-time positions declined, average wages lowered, and part-time work increased—as a result, we've been forced to adapt to these changes even with minimal unemployment today. What does adapting mean? It means we never feel like we can stop working, we're spinning our wheels to get ahead, we're delaying having kids. Some of us are working two jobs and even three—our side hustles are less about having creative outlets and more about the hustle to pay rent. Even in an expanding or growing market when we do have a full-time job, it feels all-consuming to keep it, to excel, to strive for more money and better titles.

Because of technology, work has bled into all facets of our lives: research shows that we work through our vacations, work in bed on our phones or laptops, answer Slack messages before we even have coffee or in the bathroom when we're out for drinks. For those of us WeWorkers who have created patchwork careers, they may include some level of flexibility but also take much more of our time—and often all at the expense of any sense of long-term stability.

The Social Media Trap

We don't even *really* need to talk about this other thing that defines our generation, do we? You know it all, you've read it all, your tiny pocket computer informs you of how many (too many) hours you're spending obsessing over the vacation 'grams, the LinkedIn updates, and the Facebook groups where everyone but you seems to be getting ahead.

Millennials were the first generation who grew up exposed to social media, the use of which, research has shown, is deeply linked to depression, feelings of alienation, and a sense of "not being good enough." It should be no real surprise that performing our unrealistic best lives while absorbing the unrealistic best lives of others is making us sadder and lonelier than perhaps ever before.

Social media overuse leads to distorted thinking that impacts the health of our friendships and romantic relationships—but it also negatively affects the way we feel about work, with its barrage of behind-the-scenes stories of glamorous jobs we don't have, exotic work trips we're not on, prestigious conferences we weren't invited to, promotions we didn't get, and impressive titles we aspire to but can't seem to reach (studies show millennials care about titles so much they'll take pay cuts in order to get better ones).

In theory, social media should make our professional lives easier. We have more access than ever to recruiters and mentors, can communicate with our bosses and coworkers more efficiently, and can find out reams of information about potential employers and companies before we ever send in a résumé. But in reality, social media platforms are warping our sense of how work is supposed to fit into our lives, changing it from a contained vehicle in which to earn money, to an all-encompassing "lifestyle" that defines who we are. In this way, the line between real life and work continues to blur.

Millennials are willing—and even eager—to have their work and personal lives become one, which has also led to a generation that is constantly plugged in. Our fervid consumption of the lives of others (in 2019, the estimated average time spent on social media by global users was two hours and twenty-three minutes per day, according to BroadbandSearch.net) leaves us constantly comparing our own material wealth to that of others, as we are bombarded with the clothing and gadget purchases, trendy restaurant and bar outings, and far-flung sojourns of our peers. It skews our sense of how much money we *should* be making and confuses the idea of how much money we actually need.

This new social media cost, the idea that we have to keep pace financially not only with the Joneses next door but with the hundreds of Joneses in our phones, creates a climate where we never feel like we have enough, where we're sacrificing ourselves for promotions and raises and bigger projects and extra assignments just to maintain our image on the 'gram. Whether we realize it or not, we're burning ourselves out at staggering, alarming rates to keep up a performance of who we want the world to see, but it's not who we actually are or a productive strategy to get ahead.

The Good News— Because There Is Good News

Lest you think it's all doom and gloom, all a challenging job market and a skewed economy and there's no way to get out of this, there are some positives. Because not only is this book here to help you take charge of your career, it's here to help you see what is possible, how to cope with your feelings today, and how you can reimagine and achieve your dreams despite any obstacles in your way or a world that seems stacked against you.

Did you know that researchers have found that, despite being the least wealthy generation in decades, millennials remain the most optimistic? According to a recent Gallup poll, millennials are doggedly hopeful about the future—80 percent of us say our standard of living is improving.

Sure, we've had a hard start, and, depending on our age, maybe even a more difficult middle of our careers, but our overpreparation and goal-oriented natures make us more willing to assert our big ideas. We are an innovation generation, responsible for establishing an average of 160,000 American start-ups a month, according to a study by the U.S. Chamber of Commerce. And that's not to mention that the number of women-owned U.S. businesses increased by 114 percent in twenty years, per the 2017 State of Women-Owned Businesses Report by American Express. Female entrepreneurship (which I obviously have a very conscious bias toward) is on the rise, which experts agree is good for everyone.

Study upon study shows that traits that have been traditionally, culturally considered "feminine" (though I'm generalizing here, most can be—and often are—exhibited by both sexes and many bridge the gender divide) produce better success rates in business. These traits include but are not limited to: empathy, compassion, high levels of conversational turn taking, stronger credit for work distribution, and connectivity. Not only do these qualities generally lead to more productive, happier teams, but women-led companies with a stereotypically feminine leadership style glean better monetary results.

A study from the nonprofit group Catalyst found that companies with the most female leaders experienced 66 percent better financial performance than companies that had the least female leaders. Female-led teams tend to be better connected, more collaborative, more forward-thinking, and more capable of openness and vulnerability—all traits that are highly valued in the modern workplace.

Millennials—male and female—are also changing and shaping modern workplaces in exceedingly positive ways. Generally speaking, our generation had an overwhelming amount of options—from extracurriculars to college choices—providing us with the ability to personalize our pathways at work. All that parental encouragement to not stick with something we didn't like, and instead to be open to trying new things, gave us foundational skills to start over when things aren't working out. And to not be afraid to demand more out of our employers. Research shows that millennials have pushed for more transparency in office culture, better and more frequent feedback from our managers, and more work-life integration and balance in our schedules.

What's more, our high expectations for ourselves and others lead us to seek out opportunities that align with our value systems. At our best, we desire work that reflects what is important to us—companies that value supportive leadership, that facilitate teamwork, and that devote time and attention to civic involvement and providing equality for all. If we can't find these opportunities or these companies, we've proved time and again that we are not afraid to create them ourselves.

Working women today have been dealt a complicated and, at times, an inopportune hand of cards. You may be struggling with yours, you may be ready to make a big change, you might not know exactly which card to play next. It's easy to get off track, and the most notorious career traps can keep any of us playing small.

CHAPTER 2

Notorious Career Traps

Despite our extensive educations and seemingly inexhaustible stores of passion and drive, and coaching from our hyperinvolved parents, you'd expect that young women today would be better equipped to reach their goal of a fulfilling career and a richer life with ease. However, we spent so much time listening to how we could and should pursue our dreams and thinking about precisely how to get here, we neglected to pay attention to avoiding the traps that can lead to derailing our careers.

The annoying thing about traps is that they're literally made to lure you in even when (or especially when) you're actively trying to avoid them. It's like shopping at Target. You went there with good intentions to get one thing—ONE—and left with at least a few others.

And while I really do love a trip to Target, these notorious career traps are important to understand because they contribute to bigger career challenges (aka career walls), which we'll discuss in the next section. Here's my list of the most notorious.

Career Trap #1:
Comparing and Despairing

In the age of Instagram, there's a collective tendency toward obsessive comparison. Some comparison is normal and even healthy. But when it's taken to an extreme—one in which you obsess over what others are doing or have accomplished—you can lose control of your career. This is a trap that can affect any of us at any time.

As mentioned earlier, Dr. Alyssa Westring calls this behavior "compare and despair." Her research suggests "that women's identities are more strongly defined by relationships to others than men's," which means that we're more susceptible to this trap.

The real problem with "compare and despair" is that we lose any appreciation for, and realistic picture of, the progress we've made in our career. That lack of perspective can also prevent us from making decisions that are in our best interest—both personal and professional.

It's easy to assume that everything we do pales in comparison to the curated lives we follow daily. The comparison game leaves us with a laundry list of shoulds—what we should be doing, what we should be saying, and the career status we should have by now. We're "shoulding" all over ourselves. The alternative? To enjoy and appreciate what you've accomplished, regardless of what others have done.

Career Trap #2:
"Busyness" Is a Badge of Honor

You've heard it before, you've seen it with your friends, you may have even said some version of it yourself: "OMG I'm SO busy!" "Sorry for the delayed response, been absolutely SWAMPED!"

"Ugh, can't take on another thing—I'm underwater!" This busyness boasting is a modern phenomenon. It used to be (way back in a time that I don't remember, honestly, but from what I've read and been told) that successful people worked less than others, that a mark of status was "letting your money work for you," that rich people were part of a leisure class who spent their days vacationing in exotic places and hanging out in expensive soft clothes. But today, studies show that the wealthiest among us work far more hours, have far less downtime, and are generally more stressed than their less wealthy counterparts. This may be what "success" looks like in 2020, but it doesn't feel like a win.

And it's no surprise, really. We've become a culture obsessed with busyness, with hustling harder, respecting the hustle, with the "rise and grind." The *New York Times* calls this celebration of busyness "toil glamour": showcasing one's time constraints in a way that seems performative, a status symbol, a way to signal importance in the world (it's worth noting that many workplaces embrace this busyness culture, putting unrealistic expectations on employees' time and setting goals that are unfeasible without tremendous overwork). This career trap is so counterproductive. It robs you of the time to even consider making Power Moves.

Projecting this kind of busy lifestyle has become a statement about a person's financial and social ascendency—or dominance. Our fixation and overpromotion of busyness is caused, in part, by an ever-growing gig economy where competing successfully for piecemeal work may rely on the appeal of a candidate's online footprint and personal brand, causing the line between personal self and professional self to become blurred (on social media—and in real life too).

But a busyness addiction also has to do with an aversion to and fear of idleness, of looking like a slacker, and of tying up your value in how busy you can be—even though, in reality, "busyness" is not an indication of productivity or even achievement. We even have a new buzzword for this type of busyness: FOND—Fear of Not Doing—when you feel guilty for spending free moments not being productive. This madness must stop—or we ourselves will surely stop.

Career Trap #3: Big-Picture Thinking

Another common career trap is big-picture thinking—the eyes-on-the-prize mentality high achievers are so often taught. You might know of (or identify with) a goal-oriented achiever with a five-year plan and a get-it-done attitude. They are working the system to go out after their big-picture vision. *Every. Single. Day.* But still, even with successfully tackling to-do lists, checking off boxes, and soaring through goals, they feel dissatisfied, stuck or lost, and, in their quietest, most afraid moments, empty inside.

Turns out, big-picture thinking is closely aligned with an extrinsic goal mind-set, meaning we set our sights on external achievements like fame, money, status, follower counts, impressive titles, or power for power's sake. Once we come up with a big-picture plan, our thinking around the future becomes fixed: *This is what I want, and if I abandon this goal and this vision of the future, I may become even more lost and directionless.* In setting ourselves up with a long-term North Star and starting to march toward it, we grow psychologically attached to the idea. We begin to put pressure on ourselves to achieve it, even when and if it no longer suits our needs.

After we've set a long-term goal, deciding to change it or abandon it altogether can be excruciating, causing us to feel like failures—even though this goal was always somewhat arbitrary and was set by us! Long-term goal setting often puts us in a high-pressure, external-success-obsessed loop from which it is difficult to escape. When our goals become overwhelming, when we're forcing ourselves to think about our future in such a "big" way, it can lead to a kind of achievement paralysis where everything feels unrealistic.

Needless to say, this behavior is a major career impediment. Big-picture thinking is fixed and limiting, and it often makes us lose the perspective and flexibility necessary to discover what we really want. When you're forcing yourself to think about your future in such a "big" way, everything can begin to feel insurmountable.

Career Trap #4:
The "Dream Job"

Let's face it: in your ever-evolving professional journey, one of the hardest things to give up is the myth of the dream job. I hate to break it to you, but this is a career trap extraordinaire. That's because, as much as you often know you're supposed to live in the "right now" instead of the "what if," a dream job represents a fantasy that's been hardwired into your brain since you were a kid—with all your favorite books, online articles, movies, and even mentors and professors helping to propagate this magical idea of success. It's an idea that feels comfortable, sane, and sound: The perfect job for you *must* be out there, right?

The trap of the dream job isn't just about a job itself but about the pumped-up vision of a lifestyle that goes with it. This vision includes chic-but-accessible offices, tough-but-fair boss-mentors, and stylish-but-down-to-earth coworkers with whom you can collaborate perfectly, socialize appropriately, and feature in your Instagram stories intermittently.

Much like the myth of a perfect mate, of the "one" who will fulfill your dream and lead you to live happily ever after, chasing the elusive (and nonexistent) dream job is a fantasy that takes you away from your own personal reality and distracts you from finding what it is you need in your career. In fact (somewhat ironically), when you continue in your quest for a dream job, you often keep yourself from the contentment and professional satisfaction you were striving for in the first place, as well as make it more difficult to engage any Power Moves.

In addition, these dream jobs never involve any of the harsh details about working life that you'll have to negotiate eventually but would ruin a heavily filtered fantasy: hellish commutes, absentee bosses, cutthroat colleagues, long hours, unreasonable expectations, low pay, etc. Pining for the fantasy of a dream job, as pleasant as it may be, limits your ability to experience real-world opportunities.

Even if you know that this vision of work is unrealistic, you may still put a great deal of pressure on yourself to find it, to discover that one company with that one role that will make everything fall into place. The dream job fallacy not only limits your vision for what your career can potentially be, but it's also dated and out of step with the times. Searching for one dream position suggests that you will find just a single job and then be satisfied forever. It does not factor in how you and your life will change, nor how work and industries will reshape and transform. And if you haven't gleaned this already, let me say it directly: imagining there is one job out there for you and pining for that job is part of what's keeping you stuck. At this point you might be feeling like getting unstuck is close to impossible. It's not. I'm going to show you how with actionable steps, stories from real women, and a whole slew of optimistic facts in parts II and III, but in the next chapter I want to discuss one final career challenge—the walls—before we're ready to discuss Power Moves.

CHAPTER 3

You, Meet Wall

Beyond the superficial idea of fancy titles and fantasies of what a successful professional life looks like, many of us didn't know what to expect after getting our first real job that we could call a career. As members of hustle culture, we've often worked blindly, not imagining how the pacing will make us feel in a year, five years, or even a decade. In fact, a recent PricewaterhouseCoopers study on female millennials and work found that while 49 percent of women at age twenty-five feel confident they can climb to a senior level at their companies, only 39 percent of women at age thirty-two would say the same.

This is where the wall comes in.

As we've learned already, for most women, childhoods and education systems instilled values based on "getting there"—to the Top, with a capital *T*. So you focus on where you want to end up and fixate on "making it." (I know I did.) The result? We learned to equate any stall, taking any pause in our career trajectory or any step back, with *moving backward*, making it nearly impossible to grow our careers at a healthy pace or make space to explore what we truly want and need—not to mention honestly weighing out risk versus reward. We've become overly focused on achievement to the point of obsession, and often at the expense of anything else, including understanding ourselves and our truest, nonperformative goals.

From "passion projects" to "work that doesn't feel like work," we're ruled by buzzwords and of-the-moment lifestyle trends. We aspire to be the people we scroll through on social media, watching people we don't actually know bounce from Manhattan to Paris to a beach in Bali. We obsessively monitor our peers' carefully curated money diaries and click on LinkedIn alerts about their coveted promotions and upward job shifts. We look outside ourselves for what we should be doing, beat ourselves up, head to bed, and then the next day, start the process all over again.

Our ambitions have become more centered on "I want that" instant gratification rather than on a long-term journey toward finding what makes us feel unique and fulfilled. In the process, we've lost the ability to adapt, disrupt our routines, and, ultimately, recognize any unexpected opportunities that come our way. More than ever, we need help refocusing on our own progress, on what is real and in front of us—not on the myth of perfection. This is, obviously, easier said (or read in an inspiring meme) than done.

It's important to note here that the "wall" sensation is not limited to a specific generation and especially not the twenty-five-year-old shell-shocked by their first few years in the workforce. In reality, men and women of any age, facing any significant juncture at any point in their careers, experience this at-sea feeling and wonder if they belong in the vocation they chose, and if not there, where? The quarter-life crisis is real, but so is the meltdown for a thirty-something working mom who's hitting a point of burnout, the forty-something professional who's suddenly realized that her dream career path has stalled out just shy of the C-suite, and the sixty-year-old who finds herself with ample experience and skill but who's seeing fewer opportunities, which once came her way with ease.

Like so much in life, recognition is the first step to resolution. When it comes to walls, it's the rare individual who *doesn't* hit at least one sometime in their career. So let's meet these walls before you learn how to vanish them from the career you want.

Is It Burnout?

All the way back in 1981, Harry Levinson was among the first to identify the popular term career "burnout." In his *Harvard Business Review* classic article "When Executives Burn Out," he described the condition as a "slow fizzle," a physical and emotional crisis that does not hit all at once but instead escalates and intensifies over time. These identified telltale characteristics of burnout include but are not limited to:

- chronic fatigue
- self-criticism
- cynicism, negativity, and irritability
- a sense of being besieged

The article revealed that those most susceptible to burnout had "a greater need to do a job well for its own sake than did most of their peers" and a "greater need for advancement as well (although it declined over time)." The article concluded, among other findings, that "when people who feel an intense need to achieve don't reach their goals, they can become hostile to themselves and to others."

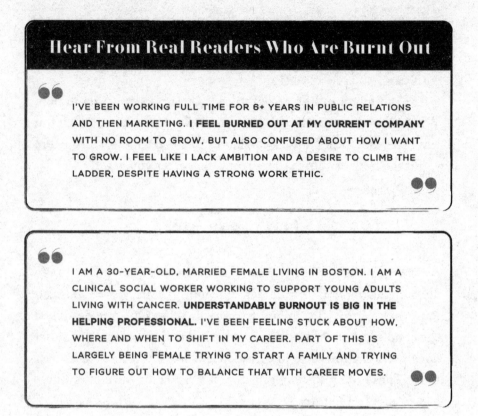

Hear From Real Readers Who Are Burnt Out

"
I'VE BEEN WORKING FULL TIME FOR 6+ YEARS IN PUBLIC RELATIONS AND THEN MARKETING. **I FEEL BURNED OUT AT MY CURRENT COMPANY** WITH NO ROOM TO GROW, BUT ALSO CONFUSED ABOUT HOW I WANT TO GROW. I FEEL LIKE I LACK AMBITION AND A DESIRE TO CLIMB THE LADDER, DESPITE HAVING A STRONG WORK ETHIC.
"

"
I AM A 30-YEAR-OLD, MARRIED FEMALE LIVING IN BOSTON. I AM A CLINICAL SOCIAL WORKER WORKING TO SUPPORT YOUNG ADULTS LIVING WITH CANCER. **UNDERSTANDABLY BURNOUT IS BIG IN THE HELPING PROFESSIONAL.** I'VE BEEN FEELING STUCK ABOUT HOW, WHERE AND WHEN TO SHIFT IN MY CAREER. PART OF THIS IS LARGELY BEING FEMALE TRYING TO START A FAMILY AND TRYING TO FIGURE OUT HOW TO BALANCE THAT WITH CAREER MOVES.
"

In the four decades since these findings were first published, burnout has become not only more common in business, but more widespread. In fact, as of 2019, it is now classified as a serious, diagnosable medical condition by the World Health Organization (WHO), the symptoms of which include feelings of exhaustion, reduced effectiveness at work, and feelings of negativity about one's work. Whereas job burnout was once mainly attributed to senior executives at the top of their game, today it happens frequently to chronic overachievers at any stage of their careers.

Burnout has been linked to depression, anxiety, substance abuse, and heart disease. It also makes us more vulnerable to illnesses—some of which can be serious. Burnout is listed as an official condition on WebMD that can impact mental and physical health. The Mayo Clinic suggests a series of questions you should ask yourself to self-diagnose:

- Do you lack the energy to be consistently productive?
- Do you find it hard to concentrate?
- Do you lack satisfaction from your achievements?
- Are you using food, drugs, or alcohol to feel better or to simply not feel?

According to researchers, burnout occurs most frequently when we're faced with any or all of the following three scenarios—which, of course, are as common as a sore throat or headache:

1. **Your job (or jobs) doesn't make sense:** If you don't know what you're supposed to be doing, if you're unclear about what your day-to-day will be like, either because you're working multiple jobs or your main position is not clearly defined, you may experience a stress-inducing loss of control, a feeling like you can never quite do a good job because the target for what is good is always changing. Erratic work makes us feel unstable, both emotionally and financially. We thrive when we know what is expected of us, when we know which goalpost we're trying to hit. Chasing work or sorting out just what it is we are supposed to be doing in a role demands our energy in a way that is frenetic and often seems unsafe—both of which are a recipe for fatigue and burnout.

2. **Houston, we have a boundary problem:** Whether it's your boss, a toxic coworker, the office bully, or perhaps a client who takes up all your time and is constantly stepping over the professional line, when the people in your work orbit don't respect your

boundaries, you will inevitably begin to exist in a heightened state of stress and anxiety. Often boundary crossing isn't just someone pushing us out of our comfort zone or not respecting our time, it can happen when we're being micromanaged by a boss or undermined by colleagues. It happens when we're afraid or reluctant to communicate with those whose collaboration, feedback, or insight is necessary to get the work done, because they might be in a "bad mood" and who knows what could happen? When you're walking on eggshells with coworkers or clients, when you're working within an unacceptable culture of fear, this heavy emotional stress will burn you out over time. Everyone has to work with unpleasant people sometimes, but when you're afraid to do your job or you dread interactions with those you work with, you know you have a problem that needs to be addressed.

3. **Your work life is (extremely) imbalanced:** It's never easy for those who are ambitious, results driven, and have access to Slack to know when to turn off the work brain and return to "personal" life. But when your work begins to bleed into every aspect of your existence, when you have little energy left to give to family, friends, interests that are not work, and even—gasp—self-care, you've not only become a cliché workaholic, you're on the fast track to burnout.

The Great Stalling

Burnout is a serious, diagnosable condition, but stalling—getting stuck, working at a monotonous job where you hate every project you're working on, where you're dragging yourself into work each day to go to a job that leaves you feeling dead inside—can bring about similar results.

Hear From Real Readers Who've Stalled Out

> I'M 26 AND HAVE BEEN TEACHING MUSIC FOR FOUR YEARS, AFTER STUDYING SERIOUSLY THROUGH COLLEGE. I NEVER INTENDED TO TEACH, THOUGH I'VE ALWAYS LOVED KIDS, AND FOUND MYSELF CONTINUING TO ACCEPT TEACHING JOBS EVEN THOUGH IT WAS NOT WHAT I WANTED TO DO—BECAUSE IT'S SOMETHING I'M GOOD AT THAT UTILIZIES MY SPECIFIC SKILLS. **I'M BORED FEELING STALLED OUT** AND AM PLANNING TO MAKE A CHANGE SOON, THOUGH NOT SURE WHERE EXACTLY!

> I'M 43 YEARS OLD AND HAVE WORKED FOR ALMOST 20 YEARS. I ALWAYS FALL INTO SUPPORT ROLES, BUT CAN NEVER MANAGE TO MOVE BEYOND SUPPORT TO PROGRAMMING, DEVELOPER, OR ADMIN ROLES. I JUST FINISHED MY ASSOCIATE DEGREE IN COMPUTER INFORMATION SYSTEMS. THE COMPANY I WORK FOR DOESN'T VALUE ME OR MY ROLE. **I'VE STALLED OUT** AND WOULD LOVE TO FIND SOMETHING DIFFERENT WHERE I FEEL VALUED.

Unlike burnout, being stalled out is quieter and more insidious. It's when you feel useless, like you're punching a clock, when you've truly stopped caring about what it is you do during your office hours, and not only is this work often a spectacular waste of time, it is damaging to our core motivation. The best thing that can happen at work is marrying our interests and values with tasks we can accomplish well, honing the skills that we care about and having the drive to improve. Stalling in a job erodes self-esteem; it leaves us complacent, uninspired, and, over time, out of touch with who we are and what we want.

Stalling out exhibits less acute stress than burnout—which makes it less risky to our health—but there is no less emotional fatigue. The stakes are lower, but phoning it in is a dull job, dims our creativity, and keeps us stuck, unable to achieve our full potential, which is work that inspires, challenges, and resonates, and that comes with more responsibility and ultimately more money and satisfaction down the road.

Here are some signs you're not so much burned out but bored as hell with your job, stalled into a rut.

1. **You're not challenged:** Most everything is exciting and engaging when it's new (the beginning of relationships, getting a puppy, etc.), and work is no different. But over time, as you acquire mastery over tasks that once seemed novel, you begin to disengage. If you don't find new challenges—and force yourself to learn new things—work will become mundane, and you will begin to feel stalled in your career.

2. **Management isn't keeping its promises:** You were told you'd be getting a promotion or a new assignment or oversight on a big project, and this never quite came through (despite your repeated requests). Your role and responsibilities haven't changed, and, as a result, you're building up resentment toward the company and beginning to hate your job.

3. **You're not a decision maker:** Maybe you were once included in important meetings with the company's change makers or given high-profile assignments, but something has shifted in the company politics or the perception of your performance. Now you're feeling low and like you're not being given work commensurate with the time you've put in or the reputation you feel you've earned.

Lost at Work

There's a third way that people hit a wall, though it's not so much hitting as it is walking around in the dark and eventually bumping into it. Feeling adrift in your career, like you have no idea what it is you want, is perhaps the loneliest of all the career crises. You've read all the career guides, the ones that told you to "find your passion"; you've bought the books and filled out the online quizzes—the ones meant to identify exactly what you should be doing, as if the technology that matched you with your Disney princess is capable of helping steer this seemingly enormous decision. You don't know which choices to make, and you don't know how everyone else seems to have it all worked out. Sometimes you wonder if you're greedy just for asking the questions in the first place. Shouldn't you just get a job and be responsible? But where are the jobs? What are you qualified to do?

Being lost often feels terrifying; it can be dignity-stealing. Maybe you think you should go back to school, maybe you should go teach English abroad, maybe you should do what the one ex who was kind of a jerk did and pack all your things and go lead bike tours in Amsterdam? There are so many options, but you feel paralyzed—you're crippled by embarrassment, angry and frustrated by your own lack of clarity. You want to succeed, you want security, but you have no idea where to even begin.

Experts call this feeling "drift syndrome," and it's defined by literally feeling adrift in our careers, not understanding what it is we're doing or how we ended up working the job we're working. Instead of plotting out precisely what should happen and when, somewhere we lost control, veering toward a job or a vocation that we have little interest in and perhaps even less aptitude for.

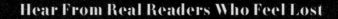

Hear From Real Readers Who Feel Lost

"

I'M CONSTANTLY LOOKING FOR A NEW JOB. IT'S LIKE I GET TO THIS POINT IN MY CAREER WHERE I START TO QUESTION "WHAT DO I WANT TO DO WITH MY LIFE?" AND ALL THESE RANDOM CAREERS COME TO MY MIND. I START DOUBTING MY DECISIONS AND THE JOB I'M DOING. **EVERYTHING BEGINS TO FRUSTRATE ME AND I BECOME SO OVERWHELMED AND BURNED OUT THAT I BEGIN TO "HATE" MY JOB.** EVERYTHING ANNOYS ME, TOO. EACH COMPONENT OF MY DAY GRINDS MY GEARS. I'M A MICROBIOLOGIST AND I HAVE AN AMAZING JOB. I'M 30 YEARS OLD AND I MAKE REALLY GOOD MONEY FOR SOMEONE WITH ONLY A BACHELOR'S DEGREE. EVERY TIME I MENTION A NEW POSITION ELSEWHERE MY FAMILY IS LIKE, "SERIOUSLY, WHAT'S WRONG NOW." MY HUSBAND WON'T EVEN CONSIDER RELOCATING ANYWHERE BECAUSE OF MY INDECISIVENESS AND HOW QUICKLY I BURNOUT.

"

"

I HAVE BEEN AT MY JOB FOR 15+ YEARS (FIRST JOB OUT OF COLLEGE) MARKETING FOR A COMMERCIAL CONSTRUCTION FIRM—A VERY MALE DOMINATED INDUSTRY. I'VE BEEN ABLE TO GROW SOMEWHAT, BUT I'M AT A POINT WHERE THE SAME PROBLEMS KEEP CIRCULATING. THERE IS A CULTURE HERE OF "DO MORE WITH LESS PEOPLE". I ALSO JUST GOT BACK FROM MATERNITY LEAVE WITH MY SECOND BABY, AND I'M TIRED AND LOW ON PATIENCE BUT, I'VE STAYED THIS LONG BECAUSE OF THE FLEXIBILITY THAT HAS COME WITH BEING HERE FOR MANY YEARS. **I KNOW I NEED A NEW JOB WITH A FRESH PERSPECTIVE, BUT I'M TIRED AND IT'S A FULL-TIME JOB TO FIND A NEW ONE!**

"

It would seem that feeling lost would only occur in the earliest stages of our careers, but the truth is, the inability to locate your direction or purpose can happen at almost any time—when we change work "cultures," leaving a job we loved and were right for to try out a bigger, more impressive company, one that may suit us less. Becoming adrift happens often when we return from family leave, fresh with a new perspective and priorities. It happens after traumatic experiences at work—the firing of a beloved coworker, when a favorite boss leaves the company in disgrace (or not in disgrace), getting passed over for a deserved promotion, when we're unexpectedly laid off and don't know what to do or where to go next.

Although we need little reminding, it's important to understand the context that can disrupt the pursuit of a successful and fulfilling career. These walls—burnout, stalling out, and feeling lost at work—can happen to any woman. In fact, research from LinkedIn Learning shows that 75 percent of us have experienced a quarter-life crisis, during which 23 percent took a career break to decide what to do next. These walls can be particularly acute for women. That's where Power Moves come in. With Power Moves, you *can* change your career dynamic. Careers are long and definitely not linear. The careers of tomorrow are still in progress. In order to build a fulfilling career on your terms, you must add Power Moves to your career tool kit, and by doing so, you'll more easily pivot and adapt when things change, reframe your mind-set when needed, and really own the decisions you make in your career.

PART II

It's Called a Power Move

As the founder of Career Contessa, I get to think about careers all day, every day. I suppose that's the definition of a passion, but it feels like more to me. I absolutely love to see women experiencing the joy and fulfillment that comes from a career that delivers what they want. Women have a lot of ground to make up, and I'm exhilarated to be part of the process.

If you'd asked me about Power Moves six years ago, I honestly might have thought it had something to do with college football. Discovering Power Moves was really more like "uncovering" a hidden superpower (that any woman could have). For me, the concept of Power Moves emerged after countless interviews and conversations, and from my professional experiences both before and at Career Contessa.

During the process, I came to recognize how much of my thinking had been detrimental to accomplishing what I really wanted—a successful, fulfilling career with purpose. Sure, I wanted a lot, but that's okay. To have any chance, it was clear that I had to update my thinking—literally rebuild my career foundation. I had to rewrite the rules I'd been taught, which simply weren't working for most women.

As I changed the way I thought about career success and accomplishments and the misdirected pursuit of trophy outcomes, I began to recognize the difference between a random Power Move and the practice of Power Moves on a regular basis. It was the difference between desperate luck and calculated success. This understanding was the final puzzle piece that helped me develop the Power Moves approach—and build resources to support this approach on Career Contessa.

In this section, I'll tell you what a Power Move is and is not. I'll share examples of successful women who have made Power Moves and, most important, I'll share what's needed to develop your own Power Moves approach to achieve the career you want, on your terms. It works because success is not a moment, it's an ongoing process. Engaging in the process and taking one step forward, however small, will make a difference. Just watch.

CHAPTER 4

What's a
Power Move?

Let's get one thing clear right away. Every single Power Move is made with the intent of helping you achieve a successful, fulfilling career—on your terms. They can be bold or subtle, grand or seemingly inconsequential, but all of them contribute to the path your career takes.

Before we discuss what Power Moves *are*, let's talk about what they are not. They are not:

- repetitive behavior, expecting a different result
- behavior guided by other people's expectations
- agreeing to do things that don't align with your personal values
- decisions or behavior driven by the need for instant gratification
- shortcuts to performing the necessary steps

Doing any of the above doesn't necessarily mean you won't succeed, but your likelihood of success and personal satisfaction is definitely diminished. There's no reason why you should expect success doing the same thing that hasn't worked a dozen times before. Working to please others and ignoring what makes you content is not a great road map for career fulfillment. Of course it's challenging to work in an environment that doesn't align with what you believe. And making decisions to achieve an immediate outcome, or cutting corners just to get something done, almost never turns out well. In all of these cases, successful Power Moves demand something different.

The challenge of defining a Power Move is that it is never just one thing—but there is a clear theme. *Power Moves are the decisions, or actions, or behaviors that make it possible to have a fulfilling career on your terms.* Quitting your job is definitely a Power Move, just like a decision to speak up at a meeting. Starting a "whisper network" or sharing your salary with your colleagues is a Power Move, just like scheduling an informational interview. Volunteering for a work assignment—one that requires a new skill set—is a bold Power Move, but no less valuable than making a habit of greeting your supportive colleagues with a smile and encouragement.

Okay, I know this sounds like everything could be a Power Move, but not exactly. Falling into a career trap is certainly not a Power Move. Doing things that lead to burnout, or stalling, or feeling lost at work are definitely not Power Moves. Being too afraid to acknowledge unhealthy habits and then allowing yourself to start over is not a Power Move. What defines a Power Move is unique to each of us. Our careers are all different: at different life stages, with different responsibilities, different required skills, different expectations—you get the idea. Taking the time to check in with yourself and understand exactly what you want can be a Power Move. Resetting your habits if/when they get off track and starting over is a Power Move. Taking an online course is a Power Move. Asking for a raise is obviously one too.

I like to think of Power Moves as: major (big), notable (medium), and daily (small). Remember, though, one person's daily move may be major for someone else. The biggest moves definitely get the most attention. They often involve a lot of thought, and their actions are likely to result in immediate change. There is no mistaking that they are major career decisions. In contrast, the "small" Power Moves might seem more routine, but they can have significant impact over the long run. Consciously changing the way you interact with coworkers or keeping a work journal are two of my favorite "small" Power Moves.

One of the great things about Power Moves is they reinforce your career direction. The more you make, the easier they become, and the more impact they can have on your career success, fulfillment, and control. Through progressive use of Power Moves, you can become more flexible, more adaptable, and quicker to recognize opportunity as it presents itself. One thing I can guarantee is that any Power Move you make with conscious intent will positively affect the way you feel about yourself.

If Power Moves are starting to sound like an approach to managing your career, I'm succeeding. It's not a matter of making just one and then returning to life as normal. They aren't a quick fix for instant fulfillment. Success with Power Moves comes from their continual use. Making them a regular part of your career tool kit is really akin to a lifestyle change.

Your career is a process, with lots of unknowns, so your approach needs to serve as a guide, not an exact road map. As you experience the power that comes from even the smallest Power Move, you'll feel what it's like to have a career on your terms. Just remember, anyone can make a Power Move (as you'll see in the next chapter). In fact, you're making one right now by reading this book! Here are some of my favorite examples of Power Moves.

Major Power Moves

- Quitting your job

- Taking on a leadership position

- Requesting a raise

- Advocating for a promotion at work

- Starting a side-hustle and/or company

- Investing in career coaching/therapy/etc.

- Asking for help

- Starting a Whisper Network

- Career transition to a new role/company/industry

- Ditching the career path you thought you wanted for what one that is truly aligned with you, your values, and life

- Re-locating you/your family

- Taking a step back in your career guilt-free

- Re-entering the workforce

- Managing family and work

- Breaking up with a friend who brings you down

- Taking time to mentor/ give back

- Disagreeing with your boss

- Removing "busyness" and replacing it with "focus"

- Having a good cry with a good friend

- Starting/growing your family

- Creating your own role in your company

- Showing vulnerability

- Taking/creating your own sabbatical

- Investing your money

Notable Power Moves

- Taking an online class/learning a new skill

- Joining a networking group

- Giving a speech/presentation

- Setting an OOO and following it for a digital-free vacation

- Volunteering for a work assignment (especially when it's new to you)

- Asking for the schedule you need to be a good employee/ good human

- Canceling plans with friends in the name of self-care

- Sharing your salary with a colleague or friend

- Investing in wardrobe/accessories that make you feel your best

- Scheduling weekly/monthly time to follow-up and/or build your network

- Setting quarterly goals with your money

- Job searching by focusing on the company first, job second

- Enlisting an accountability partner to help you reach your goals

- Creating (and sticking to) a weekly schedule

- Start a club/group at your company

- Scheduling quarterly performance reviews and taking feedback seriously

- Making a decision for YOU

- Offering solutions for large departmental problems

Daily/Small Power Moves

- Replying to emails a few days later without apologizing for the delay

- Unfollowing social media accounts that don't make you feel your best

- Speaking up in a meeting

- Saying "excuse me, I'm not done with my thought" to interrupters

- Removing self-sabotaging moves like showing up late that keep you from the results you want

- Introducing yourself to your dream mentor at that event

- Saying "no" to things that don't align with your goals

- Don't flake on the things you do say "yes" to

- Scheduling non-work fun

- Keeping a work journal

- Maintaining a bedtime routine

- Sticking to the budget you set

- Giving feedback (good and bad) to coworkers

- Saying "good morning" to your team

- Embracing that every day is a new challenge. Happiness is just one feeling throughout the day

- Owning your mistakes

- Bringing your emotions to work

- Not second-guessing/over-analyzing every decision you make

- Supporting the success of others (especially when you might feel envious)

- Finally getting to the dentist/doctor

- Prepping your meals for work

- Creating a daily to-do list

- Asking a manager to mentor you

- Setting data-driven goals

- Take a moment before replying (saying yes, no, making commitments, etc)

- Turning your phone/email notifications off at a certain time

- Not comparing yourself to strangers on the internet

- Keeping a daily gratitude list

CHAPTER 5

Power Women, Power Moves

Back in 2013, I started Career Contessa featuring interviews with real women. What do I mean by "real"? Women who are not celebrities or influencers with millions of followers (though they have amazing stories too!). Women whose stories you haven't heard a million times, who've come to their success in unconventional ways, who have a unique point of view, who represent diverse experiences and geography, who have something original/compelling/ thoughtful/profoundly valuable to say. With these interviews I noticed that these women, with success and fulfillment, had a lot in common, including:

- They were really in control of their careers.
- They were regular practitioners of Power Moves.
- Their career values were consistently similar.

While anyone can make a random Power Move, the greatest benefits come to those who embrace Power Moves as an everyday "practice" or "lifestyle" to achieve the career they want. I've asked these powerhouse women with an array of different experiences a lot of questions about power, Power Moves, and how both have impacted their careers. Sometimes (most of the time) the best way to learn is to listen to women who have been there and successfully done that and can show us what we can do with some grit, smarts, and, of course, a few Power Moves at the right time.

Gaby Dunn

Gaby Dunn

Works for   herself as a writer, actor, journalist, comedian, LGBTQ activist, and podcaster.

Previous Job   Writer and actor for BuzzFeedVideo.

Gaby Dunn is a writer, actor, journalist, comedian, LGBTQ activist, and host of the popular podcast *Bad with Money*, which debuted in 2016. She's the author of the bestselling financial advice book *Bad with Money: The Imperfect Art of Getting Your Financial Sh*t Together*, based on her podcast, and coauthor of two novels: *I Hate Everyone but You* and *Please Send Help*. But possibly Dunn's greatest career accomplishment and Power Move? A deep well of curiosity and the keen ability to adapt as her profession—writing and publishing—changed to such a degree that it became nearly unrecognizable.

Dunn got her start during college as a crime reporter for the *Boston Globe*, where she worked the six thirty p.m.–two thirty a.m. shift and used a police scanner to monitor and then chase down potential news. This was 2007, right before the financial crash, and right before journalism would move almost entirely online and into "content"—attention-grabbing headlines and clickbaiting stories.

From there, she moved into the New York media world, where she became a freelance journalist and independently launched an award-winning interview series, 100 Interviews. Since then, she's flexed her writing skills in almost every way possible—from fiction to non, scripts to novels, comic books to self-help. "I wanted to be a writer, always. When I was a little kid, I would write. And I got this award in second grade for writing, and I was like, 'I got to chase this high forever.'" Maintaining her love of writing and adapting her core skills across platforms has been a Power Move and key to Dunn's success—and also professional fulfillment: "My dad says, now because of *Bad with Money*, 'you're using your journalism degree.' Because I was like, 'a podcast isn't journalism.' But now, more people know things about podcasts, and they actually are journalism, which is great."

In addition, Dunn has consistently followed her curiosity and been willing to take risks to pursue what she wants—like moving cross-country to embark on a new dream: "When I moved to LA [in 2014], it was definitely a Power Move. I was living in New York, and I just moved here on a whim. I had this writing career in New York, which was more of a media, journalism town. And I was like, 'Well, I want to do show business, so I'm going to move to LA.' So, I just moved to LA, completely just, there was no plan, and then I've been here for five years. And I met [comedy partner] Allison within two weeks. I moved in October and by April we had our YouTube [channel]. So yeah, it was a huge risk, I think, that has paid off."

As Dunn has explored different writing genres and adapted to a changing professional climate, she's kept one constant: integrity about her work. "I don't think that I would do a project that doesn't have [social justice] in mind, or as its backbone. I'm queer, so I write queer characters, I try to have diversity and representation in everything that I do. With the *Bad with Money* podcast, I don't interview straight white men, we don't do it. I try to elevate in the financial sphere, voices that are not normally elevated. That's my brand to a T, that's what I've always done."

This is not to say Dunn's career has all been smooth or without its moments of self-doubt. "I feel lost every day. All the time. As soon as the [*Bad with Money*] book came out I was like, 'Well, we've had a good run. I guess it's over.' I cried to my therapist two days ago about wanting to quit entertainment, so who knows?"

In addition to her work on the *Bad with Money* podcast and books, Dunn continues to push herself creatively—moving from writing comedy into drama and crime fiction. In 2019, Dunn published her first comic book, *Bury the Lede*, about a young journalist in Boston caught up in a murder drama—it was based, in part, on Dunn's own experiences working as a young reporter. "It's gory, and it's a crime novel. So, I'm trying to move maybe toward scripted, even away from comedy into drama. Maybe? So, I'm never going to be satisfied is what I'm saying, and I think that's a good thing."

Julie Zhuo

"I come from a very traditional Asian first-generation immigrant family. For Chinese tiger moms, the goal is [for their kids] to have a stable career. It's like, 'You got one of three options. You should be a doctor, a lawyer, or an engineer.' Those are the three things. I felt like I was trained and taught to think ahead to really value stability—to value the sure thing," says Zhuo, a successful computer scientist and, currently, the vice president of product and design at Facebook, where she started as the first intern in 2006. Instead of taking her mother's advice, Zhuo "joined the start-up that no one had ever heard of," leading to her first big Power Move. She went to Facebook straight out of college. "I had offers from Microsoft and Google and other big-name companies, and my mom was like, 'Are you sure you want to join this college website?' Because that's what Facebook was at the time—it was a college and high school website. No one knew what it would become."

Zhuo was born in China and moved to Texas when she was just five years old. She studied computer science at Stanford and, directly after, became the social media pioneer's first-ever intern. "Going to Facebook was actually so out of character

Julie Zhuo

Works for   Facebook as vice president of product and design and herself as a published author.

Previous Job   First intern at Facebook.

for me—it felt like the risky choice. But I felt like in my twenties, right out of school, *this* was the time to take risks. I didn't know what the future would lead to, but I also knew that this was a product that I personally used and loved. I had a few friends who were there, who really loved the environment, and they were the ones who encouraged me to take on this internship and then eventually to convert to full-time. The offer that I received was lower in compensation and cash than other offers were. But I trusted my gut and it turned out to be one of the best decisions in [my] life."

Zhuo thrived at Facebook and, by the time she was twenty-five, had received several promotions and was already a manager. "I learned through the process of being at a fast-paced, dynamic place, you are going to get so many opportunities to learn and grow and stretch yourself beyond what you are capable of. Taking that leap into management, I really didn't feel prepared. I didn't feel like I really knew what I was doing. But I also felt like, 'Hey, if the company needs me to do this and is encouraging me to do this, then I'm sure I'll learn along the way, and I'll figure it out.' That was a really great and rewarding decision."

But not all of Zhuo's tenure at Facebook was quite as smooth sailing. After returning from maternity leave after the birth of her first child, she found herself lost and uncharacteristically insecure. "Everything was new and different, and I didn't have confidence yet as a mother. That lack of confidence started to bleed into every aspect of my life. Suddenly, I was questioning whether I was good at my job. I had been gone for three months. It felt like everything was going pretty well without me. Trying to come back in and again, having all these anxieties about my child, who is at home, and the transition back into work and then realizing, 'Am I really needed here? Do I actually have anything valuable to offer?' I contemplated quitting. I contemplated: 'Do I need to just get a completely different career?'"

Though Zhuo had always prided herself on being quite independent, the bad feelings reached a new low, and she decided to make the Power Move to start asking for help. She asked her managers at Facebook if she could get a coach to evaluate her work and help her get on the right path again. The experience led her in part to write her 2019 book, *The Making of a Manager: What to Do When Everyone Looks to You*, an incredibly useful book about all things leadership. "What happened was I admitted that I was going through a really hard time and the words of support and encouragement that I heard back were instrumental in helping me regain my footing.

"I also had women who were like, 'I went through this when I had a baby. You're not alone. This is normal.' I realized that we all need our support networks. We all need, especially, networks of women who sometimes can empathize or who have gone through those same experiences. That was a big learning [experience] for me. I worked to build up my own network of support. Now, [in] the future when I went through those lows, I knew who to turn to, and I knew who I could talk to, and I didn't have to feel like I was utterly alone."

Rosanna Durruthy

"When I think of Power Moves, I think of them as career inflection points. Like, there's a moment where there's a decision to be made and that decision determines the next mile of your journey," says executive Rosanna Durruthy, who's vice president of Global Diversity, Inclusion, and Belonging at LinkedIn. "For example, I had been

Rosanna Durruthy

Works for   LinkedIn as the vice president Global Diversity, Inclusion, and Belonging.

Previous Job   Chief Diversity Officer at Cigna.

working for a bank for nearly nine years. Really good job, as we're often taught we're supposed to get, and [I] was being paid well. But I wanted to do something different. That first Power Move gave me a level of confidence about the talents I had built as a human resource professional, a talent professional. I knew that I could recruit people. I knew that I could help teams solve the talent challenges they had. If a business builds a strategy, that strategy can't be realized without having great people. And I knew how to find great people. I knew how to coach great people. I knew how to work with managers to build stronger teams. I was confident about that. But leaving a steady job to go to another company, that was a bit of a risk, but I was willing to take it."

More inflection points (and ultimately more restlessness) led to positions that took her from the beaches of Puerto Rico to the streets of New York City and, eventually, into the field of entertainment, which was a role she had been dreaming about. "[After Puerto Rico], the future I wanted to create was one where I would lead a talent organization from a recruiting standpoint, ideally with a media and entertainment company. It was a big challenge for me, and a stretch, because I was now leaving the New York City area to relocate, to work in an industry that I was unfamiliar with. I stayed in that industry for about six years, until I was ready for the next risk. That Power Move was to establish my own consulting practice, because I felt I could make a difference for women, underrepresented groups, LGBT, and how they managed the career transition from manager to leader."

Once in her own practice, Durruthy began to focus her work on empowering employees and building a company culture that valued diversity, inclusion, and creating a sense of belonging. She loved the work, but it wasn't long before she became restless again.

"I had my own consulting practice for eight years, when I was ready to take on a new challenge, which was becoming part of a leadership team in a corporate environment again, but doing it at a more senior level, where I could have greater impact. So, my restlessness usually yields a new Power Move! It's almost like having a superpower. We're a big Marvel family. My kid is all about superheroes. So, I've gotten to recognize that the things I do well usually [result] in my own superpowers. My superpower is about making a bold move that makes a difference at a bigger scale each time."

In addition to her role at LinkedIn, Durruthy is an angel investor and adviser to start-ups that include Viridis Learning, Encantos Media, and Strive. She is also a former member of the HRC Business Advisory Council and served on the board of Lambda Legal. She has been recognized as one of the country's leading professional Hispanic women and an influential mind in the diversity and inclusion space. "*Success* is an extremely personal word. For me, success is being someone who makes the difference for others and making the kind of difference that people see the opportunity to pay forward. I love the word *power*. What it means to me is the freedom to self-express, the freedom to be responsible for the choices I get to make in my life, and that choice doesn't always mean you have options, but that you can own the moment and you can own what you create from that moment. I think that is the true essence of power."

Dr. Joy Harden Bradford, PhD

Dr. Joy Harden Bradford, PhD, is a clinical psychologist based in Atlanta, Georgia, and the founder of Therapy for Black Girls— an online space dedicated to encouraging the mental wellness of black women and girls. She started the organization in 2014 in an effort to combat the stigma surrounding mental health issues that often prevents black women from seeking support. For years, her main goal was to have a thriving private therapy practice, which she did, fairly quickly—but then, just when she thought her career would take a linear path, the dream began to change. Bradford began to realize she could make the most impact by not just treating her clients, but by making a Power Move to create her own media company, where she could distribute information far and wide, and a virtual database to support clients she did not have time to treat herself. It was an ambitious dream that, initially at least, not everyone in her life understood. "I remember very vividly having this conversation with my husband about starting the therapist directory. I'm tech savvy but not like a tech person.

Dr. Joy Harden Bradford, PhD

Works for herself as the creator of Therapy for Black Girls LLC.

Previous Job Director, Counseling and Disability Services at Clark Atlanta University.

Like I could not build a directory myself. So, I was going to need to hire somebody to build this directory that I had a vision for. And we had a conversation, I can remember saying, 'I'm going to need a couple thousand dollars to start this thing.' And him being very confused about, what are you doing? And how is this thing going to pay off? It hasn't even been two years since the directory has been in its current iteration, but it went from ninety therapists to over twelve hundred, so it definitely has been a huge payoff."

Over the course of launching her digital platform, Bradford also began recording a popular podcast named *Therapy for Black Girls* (just like her site)—which, in 2019, had more than two million downloads. With the podcast and with helping to produce her site's videos, Bradford effectively transitioned from being a full-time licensed therapist to more of a media entrepreneur. "So now I have a very small practice but am more full-time doing the podcast and the directory. And that Power Move [is] not something that I [ever] would've imagined, that is not at all what I planned for. I feel like I'm still kind of getting my grounding in this new business that has developed from my work."

Bradford's goal was always to present mental health topics in a way that felt accessible and relevant, but the execution changed. She now says she is living out a fulfilled career, even if it's different from the one she started with. She even has a bit of unexpected celebrity from her venture, but—as you would imagine from a therapist—prioritizes not letting it go to her head. "My support system—and really being able to stay connected to people who don't see me as 'Dr. Joy from *Therapy for Black Girls*' but just 'Joy'—has been key to my staying grounded and true to myself."

Claudine Cazian

Claudine Cazian has an objectively glamorous job. She's the current director of entertainment partnerships at Instagram, where she works directly with sought-after celebrities, along with TV and film studios, to create cool events on the social media platform. Before Instagram, Cazian worked side by side with Ryan Seacrest—from his beginnings in radio all the way into his megapopular TV shows and specials. She refers to herself as a "force"

Claudine Cazian

Works for   Instagram as the director
of entertainment partnerships.

Previous Job   Vice President of Programming
and Brand Partnerships at On Air with
Ryan Seacrest and American Top 40.

on her LinkedIn account and I'd have to agree. Cazian got her start by doing something most of us just talk about a lot: identifying her dream job and having the guts to literally go after it—even if she didn't have the "right" experience, even if she was initially told no, she knocked on a door, walked in a room, and asked for it, a process she's repeated several times in her career. It was the ultimate Power Move—asking for what you want, even if it's completely unexpected, to follow something you feel passionate about.

After receiving her master's in communication—and following a brief (and junior) stint in radio marketing and an even briefer stint as a radio producing intern—Cazian realized she wanted to make a Power Move and pivot to become a full-time radio producer, and a senior one at that. "[I knew] Ryan Seacrest was looking for a new executive producer. I remember wanting to sit down with him and everybody said to me, 'You're crazy. You're too green. This is the number one show, you have no idea what you're doing.' I said, 'What do I have to lose at this point? I'm broke. I'm living at home. I'm thousands of dollars in debt with student loans. I really have nothing to lose at this point. I can't go farther south than I already am.'

"So [Ryan] took the meeting which I appreciated, and he said to me, 'Look Claudine, I really appreciate that you came to me for this job. But you're too green. I can clearly tell you're very smart, but I need someone who's more seasoned.' I understood. Of course, in that moment, I felt like I was at a total low and lost. But as it turned out, five weeks later, Ryan called me. He had hired someone with all the experience, with all the accolades . . . and hated him. He fired him, called me, and said, 'Are you still out of work, living at home, and thousands of dollars in debt?' And I was like, 'I am all three of those things!' He's like, 'All right, I'm going to give you five weeks, and if after five weeks it works, the job is yours.' And that led to a fifteen-plus-year career with the number one presenter and host in the world."

Cazian was able to catch up her skills and learn on the job by being strategic, curious, and relentless about her Power Move to always be learning. "I asked to be in every meeting, and I sat there, and I listened. I always asked questions afterward. I asked the people above me and with more experience—what would you like me to do? And how do you want me to do it? And I think when you really *manage up* and ask the people you're working for what they want and exactly how they want it, you'll ultimately win. As long as you can deliver on that and deliver on it consistently, you're going to prove yourself to be invaluable very quickly. It's all about the long game."

The secret to her success also involved avoiding common new-job mistakes: "The biggest mistakes people make coming into a job are the following: they don't want to listen, and they don't really want to ask questions because they want to appear as if they know everything. When you're early in your career, everybody knows that you don't know everything. What they *do* want to see is you asking questions, asking the right type of questions.

Having an instinct for things and then listening, absorbing, and seeing it in action. Not just once, not just twice, not just three times, but consistently—that's the key."

After fifteen years with Seacrest, Cazian knew it was time to move on (she says she realized it during the final episode of the final season of *American Idol*, literally while watching the confetti come down), and she started sorting out what she wanted to do next. It didn't come to her immediately, Cazian says; she really had to do some Power Moves–type homework: "I asked my friends and people who have known me for years, 'What's your perception of me? What do you think I'm good at?' I was just looking for outside inspiration and the one trait that came back to me consistently was, 'You're a builder. You like to build things.' That was a really interesting word for me to hear over and over again from the people I trusted most. So, in my next move I wanted to find a start-up-y environment that had a lot of white space. A company that had a lot of room for growth, just like Ryan did early in my career. And where it was going to be a rocket ship where we could get a lot of great things done together.

"I actually saw the Instagram job on LinkedIn. I called, interviewed, and thankfully got the job. [It might have seemed counterintuitive] being in entertainment with Ryan Seacrest for so long and then being the director of entertainment for Instagram right now, which is a tech company and a social media platform. But what's so interesting is the longer you get into your career, the more you realize that your skills are transferrable, that everything is basically the same thing just wrapped up in a different packaging. So, the core skill set that you're building initially in your career will absolutely pay dividends later on—trust me."

Kadie-Ann Bowen

Executive Kadie-Ann Bowen started her career in advertising as a marketing intern at the renowned agency Ogilvy & Mather and, after this, spent more than a decade at high-profile legacy institutions like Saatchi & Saatchi and FOX before landing in the scrappy, Wild West–esque world of start-ups. In 2015, she was hired as vice president of program management at Dollar Shave Club, where she helped lead the start-up men's grooming business to a successful exit (DSC was acquired by Unilever in 2016 for a reported $1 billion) and managed not a typical corporate staff of dozens but rather a smaller team that packed a powerful punch. Today, Bowen is back in the start-up game as vice president of people and organization development at Ritual, a vitamin company named one of 2019's Top Startups by LinkedIn. The start-up life suits her management and professional style.

Kadie-Ann Bowen, CSM

 Works for — Ritual as vice president of people and organization development.

Previous Job — Vice President of Program Management at Dollar Shave Club.

"About eight years ago [pre–Dollar Shave Club] was when I was most lost in my career. I was in corporate America. I was doing pretty well. I was in a position that had a lot of autonomy. The key performance indicators (KPIs) for what success looked like were very clear. But then there was a reorg and I got a boss who was more interested in my social efforts, more like lack of social efforts. Like did I smile in the morning? Was I going out to happy hours? And I was lost at that time because I'm a natural introvert. That is not something I thrive off of. And I just felt so completely lost. I thought that I was on a good track and now I was reporting to someone who judged my performance that way."

Bowen quickly realized that this wasn't an environment she was going to be successful in—she didn't want to force herself to become something she wasn't: a super-social butterfly hanging out at after-work happy hours. She made the Power Move to start searching for another job immediately.

"[When I went to Dollar Shave Club] people were like, 'Where are you going? What do they do?' like, 'Why would you do that?' But I had a vision. I had some doubts, but I also knew that this was a time in my life that I could take a risk and if it didn't work out, I could still recover. The same thing happened with the move to Ritual. I got a lot of flak for leaving Dollar Shave Club, until Ritual's Series B was announced." Trusting her gut—and not listening to the noise around her—was one way Bowen stayed true to herself. But the top reason she says she's been successful? She makes the consistent Power Move to show people how she likes to be treated.

"I learned early on in my career that you can't assume everyone was raised the way you were or that they will see you the way you see yourself. And so, I make it really clear when I make initial contact with people how I expect to be treated. If someone says something that I find disrespectful or I don't like the way they've approached me, I address that situation right when it happens. Or one of my biggest pet peeves is when people cut me off. So when I'm talking and you start talking, I get quiet and just listen. That lets you know something's not right. And it teaches you that I don't find that to be approachable."

Another lesson Bowen learned is to replace "always trying to be liked" with "always trying to be fair," a Power Moves strategy that's useful for women in particular, who can become fixated on being likable. "I strive to be fair, not to be nice. At some point I realized, 'Oh, I shouldn't worry about if you like me or not.' It's more about 'Do you feel like I'm being fair to you? Am I hearing you out? Am I being fair to myself, rather than trying to be your friend?'"

Like many women, when Bowen first started in her career she worked constantly, had few boundaries around work, and prioritized the job over her health to a degree that she would make herself ill. "I used to be like a workhorse. I would work late. I would work on the weekends. I would not sleep. I learned my lesson when I got really sick and my employer was just like, 'Oh, okay.' That was my aha moment. I thought, 'so I'm giving you my life and all I get is "okay"?' Since then I know this: Careers are long, but jobs can be short. You have to put yourself first."

Aditi Javeri Gokhale

By any measure of success, Aditi Javeri Gokhale is an impressive businesswoman. She was the first-ever chief marketing officer of the financial services firm Northwestern Mutual—a job description she created for herself (such a Power Move!)—and applied a data-driven and creative strategy to differentiate the Northwestern Mutual brand and its products in the marketplace, also deepening engagement with its 4.5 million clients. She then stepped into a newly created role as chief commercial officer and president of Northwestern Mutual's investment products and services business, which holds nearly $150 billion of client retail assets, while continuing to oversee the company's go-to market approach, corporate strategy, marketing, and communications. Before Northwestern Mutual, Gokhale held senior-level jobs at big-name corporations like American Express, Travelocity, Nutrisystem, and Booz Allen Hamilton. And before her career even began, she moved thousands of miles from her native India to attend MIT, where she earned multiple degrees—first a bachelor's in management science with a minor in economics, and then an MBA. Like I said, impressive right?

Aditi Javeri Gokhale

Works for Northwestern Mutual as chief commercial officer and president of investment products and services.

Previous Job Chief Marketing Officer at Shutterstock.

Even with all this success, Gokhale felt like what she calls an "underdog" for a long time in her career. "I didn't have a career plan mapped for my first five to ten years, and I wasn't sure I knew what I wanted to do." Lost just out of college, she made her first of many Power Moves—instead of following a conventional or expected path by joining a company in a traditional role and climbing a ladder, she chose to pursue management consulting, which gave her access to multiple companies and allowed her to learn and try out myriad skills. It also taught her what she was uniquely good at—which would turn out to be critical to her success later on. "[Management consulting] gave me a good foundation and a glimpse into various industries. I had very fun clients—from theme parks to entertainment studios—and I found what I really like doing, which is solving complex problems, regardless of the industry."

After consulting, Gokhale went on to various roles in industries as varied as technology, nutrition, travel, and finance (she even took a career break to raise her son). Along the way, she's made dozens of Power Moves: deftly navigating her career course on her own terms; having a keen sense for when it was time to move on; and making several strategic career transitions, the secret to which, she says, is to chase problems you feel will be interesting to solve. "I have been proactive in my career, taking on complex problem-solving roles that people typically shy away from, and roles that will stretch my learning and push my own boundaries—and this is the advice I've given other women: own your career in terms of where your passion and interest take you, not so much the title and the compensation, because all of that falls into place."

One of the most important things Gokhale says she learned in her work is to fully embrace failure and understand how critical failing is to success (embracing failure? A total Power Move). "Failure should be part of your DNA. You shouldn't be afraid to fail, because if you don't make a mistake, you're never going to learn. If you fail, you fail fast, so start taking some calculated risks. At Northwestern we run [hundreds] of experiments around user experience, but many of them don't work. And it's okay. What are we learning? How are we refining? I have always lived by these three principals: work smarter and harder than everyone else, build relationships at all levels (not just with your leader), and make fact- and data-based decisions. And that's something that I encourage my leaders to implement."

In addition to her position at Northwestern Mutual, Gokhale also serves as a mentor. "I think being a female role model is just bringing your whole authentic self on a day-to-day basis. One of the things I've tried to do within my role and within my team is— I'm *proud* to be a mom, I have a twelve-year-old boy. I'm *proud* to be a wife and daughter . . . it's something that I'm very open and transparent about—with my team and with my leader. I just [try to] be a better human being than I was the day before."

Elise Loehnen

Right smack in the middle of Goop, Gwyneth Paltrow's megapopular media-empire-slash-digital-brand-slash-e-commerce-platform-slash-podcast, there's Elise Loehnen, the company's chief content officer, chief podcaster, chief cheerleader, and the person with ultimate buy-in on the message of the brand.

Loehnen guides the voice of the cult-favorite company, though she'd probably be the first to tell you it's always a team effort. A former Condé Nast girl, Loehnen worked for the onetime media powerhouse starting in the early aughts, coming into her own with a long-standing stint at *Lucky* magazine. But she wasn't always a glamour queen. She grew up in Missoula, Montana; her father was a doctor, and her mother held positions on the local school board and in the local chapter of Planned Parenthood. "My parents were very obsessed with this idea that you can't sit around. It's not done—so I grew up working."

Elise Loehnen

Works for Goop as chief content officer.

Previous Job Vice President of Marketing and Creative Services at Shopzilla.

In college at Yale, Loehnen worked in the psychology department, filing grants and paperwork, but ultimately decided she wanted to be a costume designer. "I got a job as an intern right after school on this comedy feature film, and I just sat in the trailer all day because there wasn't enough to do. I had a great time—and I loved all the women in the department who gave me the chance—but I realized this wasn't going to be sustaining for me. I ended up through a friend of a friend getting an interview at *Lucky*, which had published one issue at that point, and they were essentially looking for a freelance assistant to do grunt work.

"[The job] was all of the deeply unglamorous parts of *Lucky*, which was totally okay with me. I was thrilled to just have a place to go. So that's where I started. Just packing boxes.

"I'm a compulsive organizer, so I would stay until ten p.m. and reorganize the conference room and make myself indispensable by doing all the grunt work and volunteering for everything that came up—someone would take notice. I was operating with this idea that if I could prove to people I could be trusted with small things and make myself indispensable enough, then maybe I would get more work. And that Power Move worked for me. That's how I got my first writing assignment."

Loehnen was promoted several times at *Lucky* before stints at *Time Out New York* and *Condé Nast Traveler* and, eventually, realized it was time to leave magazines altogether. "Condé just wasn't evolving as quickly as it needed to, just in terms of how people were consuming content and understanding audience in terms of appetite. I knew I needed to stop thinking about the internet as the redheaded stepchild of publishing and learn something about it."

Loehnen relocated to Los Angeles for a job at a tech company before finding Paltrow, who had just started *Goop* as a newsletter at the time. "She [Paltrow] was like, 'I'm ready to do this—how do I scale content?' And ultimately, it took a little while, but I joined a couple months later part-time, and then joined full-time a few months after that. It felt like I was coming home.

"So many media companies are run by women, but [Goop] is different because the business part of it is also run by women. Gwyneth is an incredible boss and leader, and I have learned so much from her. On an emotional and spiritual and personal level, [Goop] has impacted my work in a way that was not what I would have ever expected to get from a job. The whole thing we're doing here is very personal to everyone on the team. It's been a profound experience."

Jennifer Gootman

Jennifer Gootman is truly a pioneer. Her current role at West Elm as the vice president of social consciousness and innovation is one she dreamt up on her own, ultimately making the Power Move to pitch the company on exactly what she wanted and why it would be beneficial for both. Before West Elm, Gootman maintained a circuitous career with one constant Power Move: she was always in the pursuit of fulfillment. "In retrospect, my career path makes a lot of sense—but it wasn't necessarily kind of a linear or laid-out path when it was happening. Right after college, I had the amazing opportunity to write for *Let's Go* travel guide, to explore the world and have that cultural immersion in other cultures—which I think served me well later in life. Now, I work on a very global team."

Jennifer Gootman

Works for West Elm as vice president of social consciousness and innovation.

Previous Job Executive Director at Global Goods Partners.

Always mindful of her needs both personally and professionally, Gootman refused to be put in a box or try to maintain any kind of conventional career narrative. Instead, she made an array of unorthodox professional (and even life) decisions, always with unwavering confidence in her ability to do good work, as long as she's doing work for a company she believes in, a Power Move to target companies that follow her ideals.

"I stayed in Spain for two years and I immersed myself in another culture before moving back to New York. I was always really passionate about working in the arts, and always wanted to have something that I ideologically believed in—so when I moved back, I started working for a nonprofit art gallery in Manhattan. I focused on communications and publication—how to pick our work for media, how to collaborate with writers and artists and publications for the gallery. But then I felt removed from the social justice issues that I care about. So, I went to work for a nonprofit policy organization and think tank that focuses on economic development and workforce development. That really exposed me to the idea of how you can—with targeted programs—make investments that improve workers' lives, improve the economy, and really make a change."

That last job pushed Gootman to do something (almost) unheard-of. She pitched the creation of a dream role to a giant company. It was a little risky, and it took time, but it turned out, West Elm needed her. And Gootman was happy to take on the challenge.

"I [was with an] organization that works with groups of women artisans all over the world and helps them access external markets. I used every bit of my career experience there. I would help design and develop products, manage the placements and ordering process with the artisan businesses, handle inventory management, customs importing, manage the website, etc. I got a feeling for every side of the business.

"After about three years there, I realized that to grow my job, I had to grow the whole company. But what if you could make small incremental changes, you know, with a large company—imagine the opportunity. Around that time, I had known the West Elm team for about a year because of our shared work in the artisan sector. So, I pitched the job to my contacts there, and started the initial conversations around what it would be like to transition. I never thought, 'I want to work in the corporate sector.' It was more the thought of, 'What's the company that's the right fit? And where is the opportunity to really have my ideals come to life?'"

The position didn't exist at West Elm, or, really, anywhere at the time. "I was connected to my now boss and said, 'I'd love to work here, here are the skills that I bring.' And he thought it was interesting, but said, 'We have very specific departments, and your experience doesn't fit in any of those departments specifically.'"

It took months to sort out the details. "This is important to say: West Elm was this ideal opportunity, but there was also a lot of risk for me. I had to turn down other offers, I had to wait. But I knew that it was the right opportunity for me."

Gootman has now been in her role at West Elm for more than seven years, and watched it expand and grow into an immersive opportunity where she has room to develop, create meaning, and, of course, find lasting fulfillment.

"I love my job. What worked for me was to ask, 'What are your passions outside of work? What are you inclined to do? Even in your free time?' Try to be attuned to your every day, and when you're happiest at work. It's really more about the little things than something grandiose, in the end."

CHAPTER 6

The Power Moves Approach

It's really inspiring to see (and read about) Power Moves in action. As examples, they can be so motivating. I love learning about them, but what works for one person may not always be ideal for you. So, in case you're looking for a single, definitive, one-size-fits-all solution to fix or direct your career, there is no such thing. Just as annoying, we must accept the fact that careers WILL change. A fixed set of rules isn't going to work, especially in a rapidly changing workplace, for needs that are individually unique. This is why I call the use of Power Moves an "approach." It describes the way you use Power Moves on a regular basis to actively guide the direction of your career—one that provides fulfillment on your terms.

Developing a Power Moves approach begins with the question, "How do you (want to) manage your career?" A lot of people don't really think about "managing" their career. It just sort of happens. Others take the "kind of, sort of" approach to career management. They tend to make decisions in response to something that's happened, usually something unexpected (even bad). Both of these approaches offer little, if any, control over the direction of your career. Personally, I'd prefer not to leave something this important to chance. The alternative is to consciously, actively direct your career.

What determines the Power Moves you'll make, when you make them, and how you'll make them—all part of your Power Moves approach—is something I call "career awareness." This term, used at Career Contessa, describes your career attitudes, knowledge, and experiences (really, everything you know) that you consider when you make decisions about your career. While anyone can make a Power Move, the more informed your career awareness, the more likely you'll make a successful Power Move with purpose and intent—one that is part of an overall approach to managing your career.

A decade ago, my career awareness was neither well developed nor informed. I didn't know much about notorious traps or the various walls. I definitely didn't appreciate how limiting my dream job thinking was. My awareness was pretty much rooted in the chase for accomplishments and milestones, and adherence to a set of expectations that didn't represent me. Even though I thought I was an active manager of my career, my awareness was so limited that the Power Moves I did make hardly qualified as an approach.

Regardless of where you are with your career, increased career awareness is the secret recipe to successfully developing your own approach—where you can make successful Power Moves and put yourself in a position to have the career you want. If I hadn't started Career Contessa and had the opportunity to interact with so many successful women and really study what makes for a fulfilling career, I might still be trying to solve this puzzle. And that's because I lacked a certain career awareness.

Shortly after launching Career Contessa, I began to collect any and all career advice. Nothing fancy, just a box where I'd throw handwritten notes, article cutouts, and printed online advice. I'd save the gems of career wisdom offered by women I'd interview, read about, or meet in person. As the box filled, and I was hearing the same items repeated, I began to really appreciate their collective experience. Their impact was noticeable. Over time, several things happened to me.

First, I identified some core beliefs that I had about careers. Mine were broad, which really helped me keep things in perspective. Whether you've thought much about this, it's a useful exercise because your beliefs are something you can always rely on when asking questions about your career. It's not a question of whether you have beliefs, it's more a question of "discovering" them or "updating" the beliefs you have from time to time. While not an absolute necessity to developing your own Power Moves approach, I highly recommend spending some time thinking about your own career beliefs. Here are mine, which might help you identify yours:

- Career change is inevitable. It's not a bad thing, it's to be expected.
- My career is unique, with challenges, opportunities, and solutions that are unique to me. There is no one-size-fits-all.
- Progress is also accomplishment. Any career move—up, down, or sideways—contributes to my career in ways that may not be immediately apparent.
- I am the only person responsible for my career.
- I am the only person who can define what makes for a fulfilling career.

The second thing I noticed—while studying careers and successful women—was an increase in my own career awareness. I particularly became aware of how my status-quo thinking was actually making it more difficult to get what I wanted. This newfound awareness led to a shift in my own behavior, my expectations, and, yes, my decisions. I started to consciously, proactively make individual Power Moves, even if I didn't recognize (yet) their value as an approach to managing my career.

And finally, the key takeaways that I'd been cataloging—advice from successful women, what I was learning at Career Contessa, and from my own experiences—became the foundation for developing the Power Moves Tool Kit. This tool kit is a collection of the things I wish I'd known when my own career stumbled. It describes the knowledge, advice, and how-to lessons that prepared me to make successful, planned Power Moves. This tool kit is the "course" that will accelerate your own career awareness and help you develop a Power Moves approach to get the career you want, on your terms.

The next part of this book presents the Power Moves Tool Kit. As obvious as each of the tools might appear, they weren't to me when I was a newly minted college graduate—or even when I was working full-time. They can reset your thinking and guide you away from self-destructive decisions based on rules and expectations that just don't apply. If you're like me, some will resonate more than others. Some might make you wonder, "How did I ever miss that?!" Whatever your reaction, I always look at them as what I wish I'd been told, and that motivates me even more to share them with you.

Now you know the path to build your own Power Moves approach. It starts with increasing your career awareness with the Power Moves Tool Kit. There's an undeniably strong relationship between awareness and better decisions. If you're aware of the things that can slow down or even torpedo a career, or affect your satisfaction, earning power, etc., then it only makes sense that you'll make better decisions with this knowledge.

New awareness will lead to a shift in your behavior, thinking, attitudes, and expectations—a more informed mind-set. You might even think of it as a new career lifestyle—one in which you will make decisions, take actions, and seek solutions that you might not have considered before. When you're doing this on a proactive basis, with goals and intent, when you're taking advantage of the power of multiple Power Moves, one after another, you're creating your very own Power Moves approach!

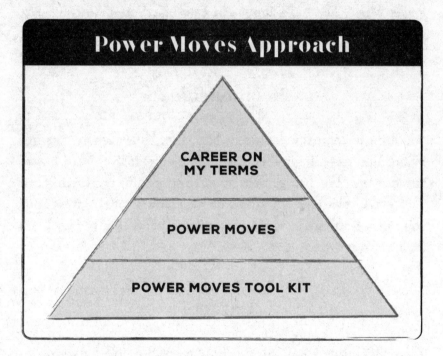

I'm a visual learner, so drawing this out was a big help. The Power Moves Tool Kit creates a foundation for career awareness. This understanding enables you to make planned, successful Power Moves (as part of your own integrated approach) to achieve the career you want. For convenient reference, I've organized each of the tool kit "tools" into four groups, as follows:

Self-Care

The importance of self-care should be obvious, but it always seems to be ignored until it's almost too late. You can't be your best and take advantage of the opportunities that come your way if you don't take care of your emotional *and* physical self. This is kind of required to make any informed, effective, and ultimately successful Power Move. The tools about self-care help you identify, understand, and own real issues that can easily hijack your career.

Relationships

You are the company you keep; hire, fire, and promote your relationships accordingly—these are all clichés you've heard before because they are 100 percent true: relationships are essential to your career progress. The tools about relationships address stuff you can't afford not to know and understand, even if you try to do it all on your own.

Career

You may already know this, but you are responsible for your own career—no one else is affected like you are. You control how you're perceived, the decisions you make, the way you respond, and the career path you forge. Awareness is the first step to successful management of your career, on your terms. Any one of the tools about these critical career issues can change your career trajectory and enable a lifetime of Power Moves.

Money

Everyone's favorite subject, and one of the biggest impediments to having a fulfilled career, on your terms. What's your relationship with money? Since a lot of Power Moves involve money, it really pays (no pun intended) to get up to speed on these tools and develop the awareness needed to establish money boundaries, ditch financial fear, and successfully negotiate for your value at work.

The right Power Move can help you deliberately overcome whatever career wall (or trap) you're facing—big or small, whether you're twenty-two and just starting a career or fifty-five and in a stall. You'll find value in the power of progress instead of focusing solely on end goals. Because success isn't about what we should be doing. It's about each of us evolving in our own careers, on our own terms, in the present moment, and without apology.

By the end of this book, I want you to ditch the circumstances and expectations that keep you distracted and replace them with a new way of thinking about your career—one that will adopt Power Moves as part of your daily practice to get the career you want. With your new (or renewed) awareness, you'll now see your career through different eyes. You'll adjust your behavior and attitudes to achieve the outcomes you want. You'll embrace the power of the process and see the value in every step—whether it's up, down, or sideways. You'll start making decisions that lead to a career on your terms.

PART III

The Power Moves Tool Kit

SELF-CARE IS MANDATORY

We've all heard about "self-care" these days. At Career Contessa, we write about it often, and one look at Instagram makes it pretty clear—it's a big deal. So much so that it's easy to misconstrue what it really is and what it can do for your life. But IRL, self-care is more than Instagram-worthy face masks and bombed-out baths. It's a discipline, a way of life that, if you practice it consistently, will change your outlook, help stave off depression, and enable you to define and advocate for your true priorities and be present so you can be your best self at work—and, more important, in life. Self-care is particularly important during times of career (but, really, any) crisis, which is when you tend to neglect yourself the most. Practicing self-care will make you capable of making Power Moves, which of course is what this book is all about.

I haven't always been the best at self-care, and for the longest time I threw it into the "woo-woo" bucket. A perfect example of this? When I first started Career Contessa, I was also working full-time at a job that required a lot of travel, training for a half marathon (which had me logging around six miles on most days), and trying to be a good colleague, employee, friend, girlfriend, sister, daughter, etc. I did not have any practice that helped me quiet my mind or live more in the present moment. I was all about overstimulating my brain and overplanning for the future.

At the end of a particularly busy fall recruiting season, I didn't make time to relax. Instead, I flew to Mexico for a friend's wedding between Thanksgiving and New Year's and wound up getting violently ill, ending with a front-row seat in the hospital. In addition to prescribing antibiotics, the doctor told me to slow down because I was very much on the path to burnout. And it wasn't just me who was fascinated by my go-go-go-ness. I was later interviewed by Brigid Schulte, who wrote a book called *Overwhelmed: Work, Love, and Play When No One Has the Time*, for a *SELF* magazine article as a prime example of why prioritizing busyness and disregarding any form of self-care is a major mistake.

So, clearly, I was wrong about thinking self-care was just some woo BS. So wrong. Self-care and the discipline it takes to develop your internal tools are some of the few defenses you have against burnout; they can reduce the effects of stress on your body, help you work more efficiently and make more thoughtful decisions, and refocus your energy. Internal tools like mind-set shifts, resilience, grit, and silencing your inner critic, as well as overcoming comparison and envy, are what it takes to secure yourself *not* in momentary feelings. You cannot develop and build these internal tools without prioritizing self-care. The other great thing about these internal tools is that even if/when you do get off track with prioritizing your self-care, you can get back on track by starting over. There are no start and finish lines that you're abiding by.

Self-care is a number of things, but the most important may be that it forces you to take a break—which, as researchers at the *Journal of Environmental Psychology* recently found, is proved to make you perform better at work. So how do you start a solid, useful, consistent self-care practice? First, you have to know your options.

CHAPTER 7

It Starts (and Ends) with You

With so many stressors hitting you every day, with your phone notifications buzzing in your pocket at a near-nonstop pace, with Slack channels dinging, emails shooting, and "taking things offline," not to mention working a side hustle in your own damn downtime, you need to find moments to be calm throughout your day, to just be quiet and present.

This is the point when most people would tell you to try meditation—which, of course, you know you should: meditation *works*. But I'm not going to do that. Here's why: You might not be a great meditator. You may not like it or want to practice it, and then you may wonder if you will ever actually be able to chill out. Recommending meditations as a stress reliever can sometimes just bring on more stress!

After meditation, the next suggestion for bringing down your stress level is always yoga. And sure, maybe you want to do more yoga, but your schedule makes it hard to find a class. Or maybe you actually hate yoga and you think meditation is pointless. That's okay! Though somehow the Western world has decided yoga and meditation are the only roads to eternal bliss, these are only two of your options for finding stillness and shifting your mind-set.

And there's another wrench I want to throw into this whole "slow down and chill" advice, which is what if slowing down isn't an option for you, *or* at least not a desirable one? Are you doomed? The answer, thankfully, is no.

Part of the reason why slowing down is hard for many of us is because we *are* living in a world where we've adapted to the 24/7 daily grind and we're more programmed for "on" than "off" mode. My goal for this book is not to give you unrealistic advice or action items we know you'll cringe at. I want to offer accessible advice, especially when it comes to building internal tools. Dr. Zelana Montminy, a positive psychologist, gets this and recommends starting with moments of mindfulness. Moments throughout your day where you're fully present can have big impacts. This can also bring you the clarity you need to start asking yourself important questions, but we'll get to that later.

And, *technically*, any time you are engaged in a soothing activity where you can breathe deeply and that does not involve a screen, you are engaging in a kind of mindfulness. This activity could be stopping at a red light and repeating a mantra while you breathe, going for a walk for ten minutes, taking a break to tend to your succulents or cook. You could lie on your floor at night and stare at the ceiling—that counts too.

A solid routine may be to wake up a little earlier each day, so you're not so rushed. Or to wake up and do a few stretches. Or, maybe, at a certain point during the day, take a short silent walk. When you get home, you could commit to a half hour before bed to engage in an activity that is not your phone—play an instrument, draw, do a crossword. Just find quiet, still time when you're not working or thinking about work *somewhere*. Building this into your day will most likely make you immeasurably more grounded, better at work, and better equipped to face your workweeks. Here's a great way to get started.

The Chill-Out Exercise

Write a list of five- to thirty-minute activities that can help you find stillness. Choose three each day and switch it up so you have variety. Try to practice consistently for thirty days.

Next, end your day with the "Ahh Pose" as suggested by Amanda Kerpius, a yoga instructor and massage therapist, for *Women's Health* magazine. "The L pose stimulates your vagus nerve, which governs your sympathetic (fight-or-flight) and parasympathetic ('rest and digest') nervous systems simultaneously." This leaves you feeling refreshed, not tired.

Change Your Mind-set, Change Your Energy

Energy is in everything we do and in order to make changes, you must change your energy. If you're working really hard but not seeing the results you want, you have to consider changing the way you currently think, act, and feel.

The Ahh Pose

1. Sit next to a wall with your legs straight in front of you.

2. Lie back as you rotate your torso away from the wall and bring your legs up against it, forming an L shape with your body.

3. Inch your butt as close to the wall as possible, using a folded blanket for extra cushioning if needed.

4. Hold your position five to twenty minutes and just breathe.

CREDIT: *Women's Health* magazine, October 2019

According to Dr. Joe Dispenza, an international researcher and author, "your brain is a record of the past, with emotions and feelings being the end product of everything you've learned and experienced up to this moment." So, if you wake up in a bad mood and start thinking about your problem coworker, not only are you living in the past because your brain is recalling a past experience, but you're also generating negative emotions.

"Those thoughts start to affect your body because thoughts are the vocabulary of the brain and emotions are the vocabulary of the body. Now, your body and state of being are in the familiar past, which leads to craving the predictable and familiar future. For example, that familiar feeling of telling yourself you're not smart enough to land xyz job leads you to feel not smart enough and the next thing you know, you're in a negative loop of thinking and feeling. But here's the real kicker—your body does not know the difference between a real experience and an experience you're fabricating through your thoughts, therefore, now the body is also living in the past because that's where your thoughts and emotions are. If you're living by certain emotions based on the past, you can't move forward and create a new future."

A new future requires that you stop making the same choices or generating the same emotions you did yesterday so you can then take action—and make Power Moves. The first step in this mind-set shift is to become aware of your unconscious thoughts and emotions. Become extremely aware of how you speak, act, and feel about yourself. To do this, Dispenza recommends that you get quiet, focus on the present moment, and ask yourself the following questions daily:

- What thoughts do I want to wire in my brain?
- What behaviors do I want to demonstrate today?
- What does it look like or feel like to be this person?

And by doing this, you're priming your brain to be a map to the future, not the past.

Eat Your Vegetables—and Other Things Your Mom Was Right About

This isn't about to become a nutrition book; however, it's important to talk about the parts of physical self-care that enable you to prioritize your internal self-care. Your brain needs fuel, and that fuel comes through food. Not all food is created equal, which is why it *does* matter that you reach for nutrient-dense foods the majority of the time, read food labels, do not skip meals or live off iced coffee, and just overall pay attention to how food affects your brain, sleep, mood, and more.

When in doubt, I find the following helpful:

- Moderation is always better than excess.
- There's a good reason for that balanced diet we learned about in grade school.
- Quick fixes and fads are exactly that.
- There's always a price to pay for too much alcohol.
- Listen to your body—don't ignore what she's telling you.

Seriously Prioritize Your ZZZs

We're not getting enough sleep—according to the Centers for Disease Control, adults need at least seven hours of sleep per night for optimal health and well-being, but 20 percent of us regularly don't get it, and an estimated seventy million people in the US have an ongoing sleep disorder.

A regular lack of quality sleep has been tied to a slew of serious health conditions, from diabetes and heart disease to depression and obesity. Not sleeping well also increases our risk of being injured, of making mistakes at work, of general tiredness, which makes us too drowsy to adequately perform the basic tasks of our days—like driving a car. According to *Women's Health* magazine, even acute insomnia—a loss of sleep lasting several consecutive nights—caused by stress because, for example, that big work project has left you in a state of hyperarousal where constant bursts of adrenaline are happening, makes calming down challenging.

So, how do you end this nightmare and prioritize sleep? Start practicing quality sleep hygiene. Here are some good sleep habits to follow:

During the day

- Go to bed and wake up within the same hour every day, including weekends. Trying to play shut-eye catch-up doesn't work well—consistency does, and it trains your body.
- Know your body and experiment with how much caffeine you can handle during the day and what your cutoff time needs to be.
- Exercise! Anytime! Any kind! Just like when you were a kid and played all day, the more physical activity you can squeeze in during the day, the more tired you will be at night. This is because our bodies were built to release energy. As hunters and gatherers we had no issue with that, but now many of us sit at a desk for eight-plus hours a day, so we must be proactive about releasing energy for better sleep.
- Avoid eating for at least two hours before you want to sleep. By consuming the majority of your meals well before bed, you're allowing your digestive system to take a break while you sleep, which in turn can help you sleep.
- Alcohol around bedtime can also negatively affect sleep—even though you may think a drink or two is relaxing, alcohol

can actually disrupt sleep schedules and cause us to wake up in the middle of the night.

Preparing for bed

- Create a pre-bed routine that includes relaxing activities like reading a physical book, coloring, and/or journaling. Limit any screen time at least thirty minutes prior to going to bed.
- Dianne Augelli, MD, a sleep medicine expert, also recommends through *Women's Health* magazine to try coherent breathing. Sitting in a comfortable position and inhaling for six seconds and exhaling for six seconds for a full two minutes has been shown to activate the vagus nerve. This can slow your heart rate and blood pressure, and decrease overall tension.
- Help declutter your head by keeping a worry list. Before you turn off the lights, consider writing down your worries, tomorrow's to-do list, and anything else that keeps your mind circulating while you're trying to sleep.

Your bedroom

- Keep your bedroom quiet, dark, and at a temperature that's at least slightly cool.
- Get your phone out of your bed. And your tablet and your laptop too. The light from any of them will interfere with your sleep and your body's organic sleep cycle.
- Unfortunately, that last tip also includes TVs. You'll sleep better once you move it out of your bedroom.

Creating the Ultimate Bedtime Routine

I know it can be easy to shortchange sleep. From personal experience, I've found the best way to combat poor sleeping habits was to create my own bedtime routine—and I'm not alone. Georgina Gooley, cofounder of female-first shave and body brand Billie, breaks up her bedtime routine to start with an unwinding ritual, which includes taking a hot shower followed by a cup of peppermint or herbal tea. Next, she likes to put some essential oil on her pulse points or spray a facial mist on her face. All of this is ritualistic behavior, but it helps signal her body that it's time for bed and it's time to quiet everything down with her thoughts.

Additionally, Gooley tries not to look at any emails when she's sitting in bed so she can really drift off. Now it's your turn. Write down a bedtime routine that includes some unwinding activities and stick with it for fourteen days. After the fourteen days are over, reflect if you're sleeping better and, if you are, how that's impacting other parts of your life.

Let's Talk About Stress, Baby

In 2019, the CDC's National Institute for Occupational Safety and Health published a study announcing that the number of American workers who identify themselves as "extremely stressed at work" was nearly 40 percent. That means almost half of those employed in the US felt as stressed at work as they could possibly be! And the number may be even worse for women, as studies have long shown that we experience more anxiety and emotional and psychological distress than men, for an abundant cornucopia of reasons, including systemic sexism and misogyny, a greater degree of domestic responsibilities, and consistently receiving lower pay for more work, along with saying yes too often as a reaction to all of the above.

This prevalence of stress in our day-to-day has mega health consequences, as the physical manifestations of stress can range from more manageable symptoms—like frequent colds—to conditions that are more debilitating like heart disease and autoimmune disorders.

Most common workplace stressors include overwork, unrealistic schedules, disorganization, boundary-crossing bosses (is your boss texting you at night? Make it stop!), interpersonal conflicts, and physical discomfort from poor work setups (girl, do you need a stand-up desk?). Throughout this section, we've been discussing the multitude of ways to practice better self-care and bring down your stress levels, but the following three coping strategies in particular may be lifesavers when you're feeling pushed to the limit at your job.

Stop Multitasking, Start "Chunking"

The ability to split your time and focus on multiple tasks used to be considered an attribute, a way to maximize the workday, a coveted trait for all of us to cultivate. However, recent research suggests that in our two-to-three-screen, always-on work culture, multitasking has become an impediment to deeper focus, to a brain-soothing sense of true completion and accomplishment. Because a stress-activated brain is a less efficient brain, our constant multitasking is leading us to feel more frazzled and fried, like our work here is never done (which it's kind of not?).

Rather than multitasking, experts on work and your brain now recommend something called "chunking"—a gross name for a smart concept—which is defined by proactively breaking the workday into large "chunks" of time as opposed to reacting to whatever inbound information comes your way (email! Slack notifications! Twitter mentions!). Remember that your inbox is not someone else's to-do list for you. Create a feeling of control over your day by setting an agenda, working on a task until completed, setting aside time to manage more reactive work like answering emails, and creating limits and boundaries around work (whenever possible). Chunking is meant to make us more efficient, as the more chunks of time you can devote to specific tasks, the fewer reactive moments you will have, which should, in theory, trigger fewer stress hormones and leave you feeling calmer overall.

Turn Down Perfectionism

The ability to prioritize both your time *and* effort level and understand when a project or task requires all of your energy versus a cursory pass may be one of the most important skills you can learn as an employee. But this distinction is near impossible to discern when you're approaching everything through a lens of perfectionism, because perfectionists view "good enough" as failure. Sure, there are certain high-profile assignments that require more focus, thought, and care, but some tasks at work just need to be finished slightly above competently and passed along. Passing something along is a really good thing, according to the founders of the Goal-Setting Theory, Edwin Locke and Gary Latham, because progress contributes significantly to your well-being.

If you have any doubt, it's okay to ask your boss to clarify which assignments are high-profile. In addition, know this: it's impossible to do everything perfectly, and attempting to or beating yourself up when you don't will only lead to heightened anxiety and stress (not to mention setting an impossible standard that will make everyone around you feel on edge too). Learn to manage perfectionism by changing your mind-set from "it has to be perfect" to "I did my best at the time with the tools that I had." Trust me, by adopting this strategy, you—and everyone around you—will be happier and calmer, and work may actually become more fun.

Complete Your Stress Cycle

While this isn't work-only advice, it can be another incredible coping tool. In their book *Burnout: The Secret to Unlocking the Stress Cycle*, identical twins Dr. Emily Nagoski and Dr. Amelia Nagoski—who have a PhD in health behavior and a doctorate in musical arts between them—argue that we lead lives humming with stress, but we never complete the "stress cycle." A stress cycle is the moment when our bodies learn that after facing danger, we are now safe. When you reach "safety," you have completed your full stress cycle.

Since we no longer have to run away or protect ourselves from wild animals, let's use a modern example. When Chris in finance calls out your mistake in front of the whole team, when you're leading a huge project that's behind schedule, when the presentation to your board is met with indifference, or when any other stressful work example you can think of takes place, your cortisol and adrenaline spike. When this stress response happens on the daily, it can lead to chronic activation, as the Nagoskis note. This chronic activation can lead to high blood pressure, slowing down your gut function and more. A solution is to complete your stress cycle. Here are five ways the Nagoskis recommend that you can de-stress and complete your stress cycle.

1. **Social interaction:** Casual interaction with your crew is the first sign that the world is a safe place.
2. **Laughter:** Laughing or thinking about funny times increases relationship satisfaction. When was the last time you had a deep belly laugh?

3. **Affection:** If the above are not cutting it, deeper connection with a loved one might be what you need. The Nagoskis say that "it doesn't have to be physical affection, though physical affection is great; a warm hug, in a safe and trusting context, can do as much to help your body feel like it has escaped a threat as jogging a couple of miles, and it's a heck of a lot less sweaty."

4. **Crying:** Finally, the proof we all know is true—a good cry can solve stress! The sisters write, "Have you had the experience of just barely making it inside before you slam the door behind you and burst into tears for ten minutes? Then you wipe your nose, sigh a big sigh, and feel relieved from the weight of whatever made you cry? You may not have changed the situation that caused the stress, but you completed the cycle."

5. **Creative expressions:** When you're going through your creative outlet, your big emotions can be expressed. The Nagoskis also add that: "Engaging in creative activities today leads to more energy, excitement, and enthusiasm tomorrow."

These are just five ideas to consider and only you know what you truly need to complete your stress cycle; however, now you know that crying at work might be just what you need for a very legit reason.

From your mind-set to your bedtime to completing your stress cycle, prioritizing your self-care must play a major role in your life. Prioritizing yourself is not selfish, it's smart. Otherwise, you'll find it very challenging to deal with the other important parts of your life. To help, here's a quick recap on where to start:

- Find simple ways to bring mindfulness into your day-to-day by repeating a mantra while stopped at a red light, going for a silent walk for ten minutes, taking a break to knit or cook, or even just breathing deeply for three minutes a few times per day.

- A new future requires that you stop making the same choices or generating the same emotions you did yesterday. The first step in this mind-set shift is to become aware of your unconscious thoughts and emotions. Become extremely aware of how you speak, act, and feel about yourself.

- Create—and stick to—a well-rounded approach to your diet, as well as a consistent bedtime routine that includes banishing electronics as far from your bed as they can be.

- If your workload is stressing you, try something called "chunking" by proactively breaking the workday into large "chunks" of time as opposed to reacting to whatever inbound information comes your way. Chunking makes us more efficient at work, which can help trigger fewer stress hormones.

- Turn down the perfectionism by changing your mind-set from "it has to be perfect" to "I did my best at the time with the tools that I had."

- Determine what you need to complete your stress cycle so you can de-stress for good.

CHAPTER 8

Treat Your Intuition Like Your New Best Friend

Self-care isn't just about cultivating good physical habits; you need to pay attention to your emotional life too. That means learning to trust yourself and your instincts so you can feel empowered and confident enough to make important decisions on your own.

Even with some prep work, I still relied heavily on my intuition to help me launch Career Contessa. I didn't create a fully outlined business plan or raise a round of funding from outside investors. I was trusting my instincts to make my first big moves, which included investing my time, energy, and resources into creating high-quality, consistent content—even though I had no background as a content creator and wasn't sure how being a media-heavy resource company would benefit us.

My first step was to determine the type of content we would create, and when I spoke to all the "experts," they recommended I cover lifestyle content and then add in career advice every once in a while because no one had an interest in reading only about careers. And for the first year, I did do that. We wrote about our favorite summer sandals and lunches you could pack for work. But my intuition knew that this wasn't us. It wasn't what Career Contessa was about.

Once I stopped producing lifestyle content and focused only on career advice, I saw major growth in our audience. And that same career-specific content is what helps us stand out in a crowded space with a unique offering. Going against the advice of the "experts" can seem almost dangerous at times, until you realize that no one *really* knows what they are doing.

There's a reason why most success stories involve shutting down the haters and taking a big freaking risk based on what your gut tells you to do. Actually, science tells us this is true too. In 2008, researchers confirmed that "gut feelings" are based on drawing from past experiences and observations instinctively—so quickly that you may not even sense where you're getting those feelings from. And so your hunches are acting in your best interests. Sounds great, but how do you get back to trusting yourself and actually listening to that voice inside your head?

In his book *Sources of Power: How People Make Decisions*, cognitive psychologist Gary Klein outlines how your intuition works, by processing four different kinds of information:

1. **Relevant cues:** Intuition makes the job of sorting out an unfamiliar situation less strenuous because it narrows down the stimuli you're receiving, gives you relevant cues, and teaches you what you should focus on.
2. **Expectancies:** Intuition answers the question: What should I expect? It helps you understand a situation before you even enter it.

3. **Plausible goals:** Intuition also lets you in on the plausible goals you'll want to have in any situation, like if you're unexpectedly in a meeting with someone who has the power to improve your career, your intuition will know and let you in on the goal to impress this person.
4. **Typical actions:** Finally, intuition suggests actions to you. It's thinking faster than you; it will tell you what to mention to the person you want to impress.

All of these together help guide you through your life, and by trusting your intuition, you will leave yourself open to take more risks, choose the less conventional path, and go after what you want. It's like having a bit of a superpower—you just need to get calm and courageous enough to use it because ultimately this is asking you to change your behavior, which is not an easy ask, but these *are* the actions that help you evolve.

The Mini-Risk Challenge

1. Begin by writing a list of things that give you the most anxiety (e.g., saying no to a pushy coworker or speaking up at a meeting).
2. Next, write down a goal that will help you push through this anxiety (e.g., "I will tell James when he comes by, *again*, that I can't chat because I'm on deadline, and I won't apologize" or "I will volunteer an idea or question in this Tuesday's team meeting").
3. From the initial list, choose three risks to take in the next week.

Research shows that our intuition is not some new age fiction, but a real tool that can help us know ourselves better and survive and thrive at work (and in life). When you learn to trust yourself and your instincts, you will feel more empowered and confident enough to make important decisions on your own. By trusting your intuition, you may become open to taking more risks, choosing the less conventional path, and going after what you want most profoundly and fundamentally.

CHAPTER 9

Cut the Subliminal Self-Loathing

For women, worrying about "growing up" and how this whole life thing is going to work out isn't totally illogical or unreasonable. If we want to find a life partner, we sense that we have a finite window of time to make sacrifices in our personal lives in favor of focusing on our careers. If we intend to have children, there's another clear deadline in our minds—we need to advance our careers as far as possible before we take a career break. Thanks to many of our obsessions with the rigid plans, discussed in Part I of this book, we focus on getting to a preplanned point before a certain age. We internalize those ambitions, constantly visualizing ourselves in roles (the "When I grow up, I'm going to be a [insert specific title here]") that we've planned for since we were in our teens.

Then, suddenly, we find ourselves thinking, "I'm twenty-eight years old, and I haven't even made director yet. I've failed." You start quietly hating yourself for not achieving some invisible or unrealistic goal. The pressure may be unconscious—ghost pressure— but you often feel bad about it and disappointed in yourself and you can't quite pinpoint why. You're subliminally self-loathing for something you haven't even done wrong! The problem here is that you're focusing, consciously or not, on what you've been idealizing for years rather than thinking about what the you of today actually wants. In other words, you focus on the career plan and not the career vision.

Instead of embracing the process—and really thinking about how and where you want to be, not where you expected you'd be or (worse) where others expect you to be—you obsess about how time is running out. You've grown up, and you're not where you "should be." In order to get out of this mind-set, you need to stop hyperfocusing on the future, learn to live in the unknown, and be where you are today. One of the best ways to do that? Silence your inner critic.

Silence Your Inner Critic

In the beginning of my career, I was afraid of public speaking. I declined the opportunity to present at meetings and wasn't confident I wouldn't stumble over my words. While working as a volunteer for the Make-A-Wish Foundation, I was asked to guide a group of influential donors around an event. I immediately choked up and recommended another volunteer who would be a better fit for the job as my excuse to bow out. When I got in my car later that night, I started to cry for not having been brave enough to take on the opportunity to network with "those" people. Beating myself up for my public-speaking fear resulted in more negative self-talk, which ultimately became a self-fulfilling cycle that I struggled to overcome.

For longer than I'd like to admit, I lived in this cycle where my best way to cope with disappointment and the unknown was to be really hard on myself, and I would invite my inner critic and ego to battle it out with my inner voice. Some of you might relate to this pattern, and if you do, then you know that Ms. Inner Critic KO'd my inner voice—*Every. Single. Time.* My pattern looked like this:

1. **I start to spin:** Something would not go according to plan—I wouldn't get results I was striving for—and I would fall into my own ambition trap.
2. **My inner critic starts:** In order to cope with this disappointment and motivate myself to do better in the future, I would listen to my inner critic telling me I'm not good enough and all the ways I messed up, and retreat to isolation—or call my mom (moms can be incredibly soothing in a meltdown) to help motivate myself to get back up and work even harder.
3. **The shame and self-doubt are poured on:** This pattern would dropkick me into a place of self-doubt that I would then need to dig myself out of.

This pattern was a coping mechanism for me, however, when I saw that Make-A-Wish volunteer turn her networking efforts into an amazing full-time job, I knew I had to make a shift to stop limiting my professional opportunities. That's around the time that I started to volunteer at work to give tours to potential students, which required improvisation. I also supported team meetings and the heads of faculty with specific admissions programming. I even enrolled in a communications graduate class, with the final assignment being a public speaking presentation where I received great feedback. When I started to feel more comfortable with public speaking, I realized my old pattern was far from helpful and that perceptions of myself were really the thing creating my professional ceiling.

It's taken me about a decade of messing up, making gutsy moves, and going against my risk-averse tendencies to see that no part of my pattern was helpful or productive. Instead, I was sending myself a few steps back on any progress I was making each time I entered this cycle. It's also taken some therapy and talking to many women, specifically life coach and author Christine Hassler, about similar feelings to realize that not having all the answers—and embracing that uncertainty—is completely doable, by learning how to silence (or at least work *with* and not against) your inner critic. According to Hassler, here's how you can do that:

1. **Start by loving and accepting your inner critic:** Anything that you resist will persist, and your inner critic is not all bad because you often *are* more motivated when you're harder on yourself. There's a therapist part of your inner critic that thinks she's serving and protecting us. Therefore, criticizing the inner critic is just going to send you into a downward spiral because first you feel the inner critic come up, then you criticize, and it leads to a one-way ticket to the criticism party.

2. **The number one way we start to break patterns is to observe:** Let's say that after a phone interview you hang up and say, "I stumbled over my words. I didn't sound smart. That was stupid. They'll never pick me," etc. Your inner critic really rears her protective head, but this time you'll respond with, "Hello, inner critic. There you are, helping to protect me. I understand that you come up because you're committed to me doing the best I can, so how about we just take on more of a coach role instead? I want to promote you to be a coach rather than just a critic."

    This internal conversation might seem silly, but researchers—including Tamar E. Chansky, PhD, author of *Freeing Yourself from Anxiety*—have linked negative self-talk to higher stress and lowered self-esteem, and studies suggest that overcoming negative self-talk and learning to be more gentle and even optimistic with ourselves can lead to myriad health benefits, such as lower rates of depression, lower levels of stress, better coping skills, and even a stronger immune system.

3. **Don't jump to becoming a cheerleader:** After you've promoted your inner critic, you can respond with, "I did my best, and I'm going to review how I can prepare more in the future." You don't want to go from beating yourself up to saying, "I nailed it," and telling yourself, "I'm the best phone interviewer ever." You don't need to jump to suddenly affirming yourself in a colossal way, because the brain and the psyche can't make that big of a pendulum swing.

4. **See if you can just be a bit kinder:** The way you work with the inner critic is by promoting her and seeing if you can be a bit kinder so that it starts to shift your pattern. The more you can observe and talk to that part of yourself rather than letting her run her course or trying to use criticism to manage her, the more you're going to have a relationship with your inner critic that doesn't feel as self-defeating.

5. **And as a bonus tip, name her:** Since you're going to potentially be doing a lot of talking to your inner critic, it's helpful to also name her so you really do feel like you're talking to a third party that you *can* control. Mine is "Kari"—appropriately named after an elementary school bully I had.

To jump-start your new practice of speaking more kindly to yourself, I recommend creating a mantra that you can recite each day. This is especially helpful in challenging moments. If you're already doubting if this can work, hear me out. I wrote a mantra and taped it to my car dashboard and then said it aloud five times on my way to work for thirty days straight. While no one hooked me up to a lab to track how this affected my brain, emotionally I felt better after a consistent practice, and in the end, how I feel is what really matters. Here's how you can create a mantra of your own.

Self-Love Mantra Making 101

Teach yourself mantras that make you feel safe and grounded in this moment, such as:

- "This moment is good just as it is."
- "I appreciate myself as I am, where I am."
- "My goal is to grow stronger, smarter, and braver, not to achieve an external reward on a timeline."

Write down a self-love mantra for yourself and put it somewhere you'll see it daily, like your car, your desk, the refrigerator, etc. Anyplace where you can see it and downshift your mind to focus on this mantra.

The number one way we start to break unhealthy patterns is to observe, so start observing any time you are practicing self-critical talk and be aware of when and why you do it. This awareness alone will help you stop. Remember, learn to love and accept your inner critic—you may even want to give her a name—and teach yourself self-love mantras that make you feel safe and grounded in the moment.

CHAPTER 10

Get Your Mental Health House in Order

Self-doubt. Anxiety. Overthinking. Impostor syndrome. Shame spirals. At one point or another, we've all been there—and will be there again. We've all let lapses in self-worth and solid boundaries or taking care of our mental health sabotage our work, make us feel like we don't belong, like we don't deserve achievement, like we should pack up our toys, leave the sandbox, and go home.

Work has the capacity to bring out some of our best qualities— empathic leadership, kindness, collaboration, innovation—but it can also trigger some of our worst, most self-destructive ones too. The ability to address your emotional and mental health needs, so you can be present and effective on the job and so you can stop getting in your own way, is likely the most important self-care you'll ever learn or practice. This enables you to gain clarity and direction for future Power Moves, particularly when you're lost or stuck, or experience feelings of uncertainty or low self-worth.

Getting your mental health house in order is therefore an imperative, not a nice-to-have, more crucial to your satisfaction and survival than nearly anything else. It goes beyond simple self-care routines to developing a sense of groundedness and core strength that includes both understanding your limits and exercising self-control, along with knowing when to sound the alarm and seek help, free of shame.

If you're struggling to feel grounded and being weighed down by feelings of exhaustion, stress, anxiety, and more, it might be time to consider taking a mental health day. Mental health days are occasional days off from work that allow you to recharge and focus on your well-being. Growing up, my mom would let my sister and me take mental health days, which really just meant we could tell her we wanted to stay home from school because we "weren't feeling it." As an adult, it's important for you to create space when you're not feeling it as well.

When to Take a Mental Health Day

Now that you know you can and occasionally should take a mental health day, it's time to figure out the right timing. According to Career Contessa contributor Justine Figueroa, before you take a mental health day, ask yourself these questions:

1. Are you unable to pinpoint where your distress is coming from? Or is it directly related to an upcoming deadline or presentation?
2. Do you have a big project or meeting coming up? Are your coworkers depending on you for something soon?
3. Are you starting to resent the job you once loved?

If you think your stress and worry are related to big projects and will likely fade away once you've finished them, try to hold off on taking a mental health day until after the project is completed, so no one is left waiting for you. Plan a mental health day during a time when you're not essential to the day-to-day activities in your office. It will give you something to look forward to and will motivate you to push through your work.

If you don't understand where these unsettling feelings are coming from and you're starting to dread heading to the office every day, it might be time to seek the advice of a professional. Beyond serious and/or debilitating mental health illnesses, like anxiety (which is so prevalent it impacts forty million Americans each year), there's an array of emotional hazards or symptoms that trip us up during the daily nine to five.

If you're suffering from depression, severe anxiety, compulsive behavior, or panic, or if things just don't seem right, take the actionable steps you need to get the professional support you deserve. If your arm was broken, you wouldn't think twice about going to a professional. Your mental health is no different. Try to think of therapy as an opportunity for learning, the chance to better understand yourself and the things you do, so you can value yourself more. One of my favorite Diane von Furstenberg quotes is "The most important relationship you have in life is the one you have with yourself." You need to always remember that. I've gone to a therapist on and off for about a decade, and I can confidently share that it's been one of my best decisions as I continue to prioritize my relationship with myself.

Start valuing your emotional and mental health needs to the same degree that you value other parts of your life—and reframe how you consider addressing them. Getting professional treatment for mental illnesses, asking for emotional assistance, creating a healthy outlet, joining a support group, or even finding a confidant to share with are all great options to consider.

Lean into Resilience—
and the Problem with Happiness

Contrary to popular belief, resilience is about the reboot—not the hustle. Hustle culture on Instagram has led us astray because hustle without flow just doesn't work. You can fall and get right back up again, but if you haven't taken the time to reflect, what's the point? One of the hardest parts about a transition is that while it's the start of something new, you also have to come to an end with something else, which is why you shouldn't just hustle to the next thing.

When I transitioned from Hulu to Career Contessa, it was hard not just because I had a lot of people doubting my decision, but because I was afraid too. I had worked so hard to get to Hulu, loved my job, and I was scared about how this next move would work out for me. Not everyone will be on your team when you're making a Power Move, but you have to be strong enough to do it without their buy-in. That first year of full-time entrepreneurship was full of ups and downs—some even in the same hour—but with each fall and each low moment, I kept building. I kept trying, and I continued to keep learning and iterating along the way.

The reboot is how you're able to pause, and taking care of yourself is such a critical part of managing daily stressors—including the one that makes us think we're striving for 24/7 happiness.

We are so obsessed with happiness in our culture that it's actually making us really unhappy. We have read all these happiness books and listened to the folks talking about happiness, yet we live in one of the least happy developed countries in the world. Happiness is a fleeting feeling that comes and goes. We can feel happy a hundred times a day if we're able to capture that happiness, but we can also feel unhappy at any point, and that's okay too.

There's something that exists—sometimes as a companion to happiness and sometimes in its absence. It's contentment. Unlike happiness, contentment is the state of existing in your current day-to-day. Contentment is closer to balance. It's felt by experiencing those moments of dissatisfaction and leaning into them instead of shunning them. It's reflecting, in moments of despair or desire, on what you do have and how that can feed into your long-term success. Use contentment as a tool to carry you through your moments of sadness, disappointment, or bitterness.

I've personally found that when I embrace feeling unhappy—like being sad, disappointed, angry, etc.—I feel better. Being okay with unhappiness is hard for many of us because we've been programmed to believe that not only is a constant state of happiness achievable, it's the goal. However, if we anchor our goals in a fleeting feeling, it sets us up for unhappiness, so why tie your anchor to that boat to begin with?

Analysis Paralysis—Overthinking Kills More Ideas Than Failure

You've probably heard of analysis paralysis, the state of overthinking every single outcome of a potential situation to a degree that you become unable to make decisions on your own. The seeds of analysis paralysis usually begin with some combination of the following: worrying if you've shown up correctly, if the person you were talking to understood what you were saying or took things the "wrong" way, about scenarios over which you have little control.

This lack of control makes you feel terrified and starts your brain spinning.

Analysis paralysis is all too common. It can impact your ability to self-advocate, manage conflict, walk away from a bad situation, and lead effectively, and can even make you miss out on potentially amazing opportunities. In effect, overthinking can impact every single aspect of working life, getting in your way and keeping you from success more often than you think. Inaction can be crippling in any business based on timeliness or deadlines; as a leader, it can make you seem weak or unreliable, and as a worker out there hustling for gigs, it can hurt your chances of representing yourself and competing effectively.

When you're stuck in this state, when you're trying to game out every possible outcome, every minor and major way that it could all go wrong, when you're projecting all kinds of negative thoughts onto coworkers and bosses, you will stay inactive, fixed, suffocated, and unable to think about or take action on priorities or goals. Overanalyzing will leave you lost and will prohibit you from ever even attempting a Power Move, much less executing one! Here are a few suggestions to combat overthinking:

Acknowledge Your Feeling

The best way to overcome a state of analysis paralysis, according to Career Contessa contributor and licensed counselor/career coach Nancy Jane Smith, is to first acknowledge how you're feeling. Notice when your body begins spinning out for no reason. Acknowledge precisely what it is you are experiencing in your body and feeling in your mind. Scared? Angry? Insecure? Getting into your body and naming your feelings with concrete words will help ground you and keep you from spinning out of control.

Overthinking Problem	Power Moves Solution
THERE ARE TOO MANY OPTIONS	DEVELOP A CREATIVE, ENGAGING SYSTEM FOR NARROWING YOUR DECISIONS – A PERSONALIZED POINTS METHOD OR A CHART THAT BACKTRACKS FROM WHERE YOU ULTIMATELY WANT TO BE AND HOW THESE DECISIONS MIGHT TAKE YOU THERE.
YOU HAVE LITTLE CONFIDENCE IN YOUR ABILITY TO MAKE THE "RIGHT" DECISION	CREATE A MANTRA FOR CONFIDENT DECISION MAKING, SOMETHING LIKE "NO ONE KNOWS WHAT'S BEST FOR ME BETTER THAN ME"
YOU'RE OVER-COMPLICATING A SIMPLE SITUATION	STRIP THE SITUATION DOWN TO ITS BAREST PARTS, TAKE OUT CONJECTURE, SPECULATION, AND ANYTHING THAT IS NOT A FACT.
YOU WANT TO MAKE THE PERFECT DECISION SO YOU ARE OVER-RESEARCHING AND STALLING MAKING ANY DECISION AT ALL.	REMEMBER THAT PERFECTION IS A FANTASY AND GIVE YOURSELF A FIRM DEADLINE TO COME TO A CONCLUSION AND A LIMIT FOR HOW MUCH RESEARCH YOU WILL ALLOW YOURSELF TO DO.

Slow Down

Smith also suggests that all of the meditation tricks will work here as well: slowing down, deep and focused breathing, simple stretches, something silly like dance—just getting out of your head in any way. For me, I like to walk and listen to a podcast that's about anything *other* than work—murder mystery, history, and lifestyle topics are my go-to distractions. By returning to your question outside of a heightened emotional state, you allow yourself to more calmly make a decision. You'll understand in a bigger-picture way that you can accept whatever outcomes your decision brings.

The Five-Minute Rule

I once received some great advice to set a time limit rule. You can talk about that "thing" nonstop for five minutes, and then you have to let it go for that day. Talking about something over and over *and* over again (especially in the same twenty-four-hour period) just leads to more overthinking. And as they say somewhere in an inspirational meme on Instagram, "What will people say?" has killed more dreams than failure ever could.

When it comes to getting your mental health house in order, taking a first step is key. In addition to serious mental health conditions, recognize that forcing yourself to bounce back to the hustle or overthinking things to a point where it leaves you unable to make decisions are also conditions to take seriously. There's nothing wrong with you for having these experiences— it's only wrong if you try to sweep them under the rug instead of creating healthy coping mechanisms.

Battles with mental health can be insidious. If you are struggling with feelings of exhaustion, stress, and anxiety, here are a few resources to help from the National Alliance on Mental Illness (NAMI):

- HelpWhenYouNeedIt.org features over 350,000 listings for social services, mental health, substance use, legal, and financial assistance.
- *Psychology Today* offers a national directory of therapists, psychiatrists, therapy groups, and treatment facility options.
- Anxiety and Depression Association of America (ADAA) provides information on prevention, treatment, and symptoms of anxiety, depression, and related conditions (240-485-1001).
- National Institute of Mental Health (NIMH) provides information on statistics, clinical trials, and research. NAMI

references NIMH statistics for their website and publications (866-615-6464).

- HealthCare.gov provides specific information about coverage options in your state, including private options, high-risk pools, and other public programs (800-318-2596).
- Depression and Bipolar Support Alliance (DBSA) provides information on bipolar disorder and depression and offers in-person and online support groups and forums (800-826-3632).
- International OCD Foundation provides information on OCD and treatment referrals (617-973-5801).
- National Eating Disorders Association (NEDA) provides up-to-date, reliable, and evidence-based information about eating disorders (800-931-2237).
- Schizophrenia and Related Disorders Alliance of America (SARDAA) offers Schizophrenics Anonymous self-help groups and toll-free teleconferences (240-423-9432).
- Sidran Institute helps people understand, manage, and treat trauma and dissociation, and maintains a helpline for information and referrals (410-825-8888).
- Therapy for Black Girls is an online space dedicated to encouraging the mental wellness of Black women and girls founded by Dr. Joy Harden Bradford. Easily find and book a therapist online (www.therapyforblackgirls.com).

CHAPTER 11

The Shame Game Is a Losing Game

No conversation about self-care, mental health, or just simply being and feeling emotionally well would be complete without a discussion around shame. Shame—highly potent feelings of inadequacy, regret, humiliation, disconnection, or unworthiness—is among the most common negative emotions humans experience. At work, shame is the source of many of your most ill-advised decisions, inappropriate reactions, career blocks, stumbles, and fears. Shame can be all-encompassing, escalate quickly, and lead to actions that leave us with deep and lasting regret.

It is frequently confused with embarrassment—but whereas embarrassment occurs rapidly and passes swiftly, shame can linger for decades, even a lifetime. It can pop up unexpectedly, be triggered by seemingly disconnected events. Shame doesn't just make you think you've done something wrong; it is so powerful that it forces you to believe that you yourself are fundamentally wrong. It binds to the rest of your feelings and can expand until it feels like it's touching everything you do.

So how can you overcome a force so powerful and destructive it

can utterly block your path to professional (and personal) fulfillment, set up camp in your brain, and stay in your way? First, you
need to create an environment where shame is unable to thrive.
This may be easier and more logical than it sounds—at least in
theory. According to author, researcher, and advice powerhouse
Brené Brown, shame requires three things to survive: silence,
secrecy, and judgment.

Which means the next time you're feeling ashamed, you may
have to do the thing you probably *least* feel like doing, the thing
that feels the hardest: find a way to talk about it, in a psychologically safe environment, with someone you can trust. "The less we
talk about shame, the more power it has over our lives," Brown
explains in her book *Daring Greatly*. "If we cultivate enough awareness about shame to name it and speak to it, we've basically cut it
off at the knees."

Shame at work usually springs from underperforming, letting
yourself down, and exhibiting behavior that doesn't align with
your core values and ideals. But shame also happens when we work
in emotionally toxic environments around people who make us
feel unsafe. If the latter is happening to you, this is most likely
the issue to address first—by identifying the problem and understanding that not only do you have value and are worthy but that
you deserve better than a destructive workplace, and then taking
initial steps to change your circumstances (this is not easy work,
and it won't happen overnight, so be gentle and kind to yourself
as you begin to work through the process).

If it's the former, and there's behavior of your own you seek to
change, the more you can learn to accept your mistakes as opportunities, the more you learn that failure can actually be amazing
and lead to better things, and the more you can see yourself as being on the path to learning and evolving, the less you will continue

to judge yourself. And once you start being open and transparent about what makes you feel ashamed (to people you can trust) and then start accepting your actions as just part of the process without judgment, shame will no longer have a place to hide. I once listened to a keynote conversation with the president of a major university, and she said her best advice to other women is to learn how to not take things personally, because that will serve us better than responding to every reaction—including the ones we make up in our heads. Or to get very woo-woo and quote a common internet proverb: "When there's no enemy within, the enemies outside can't hurt you."

The following are some ways to talk to yourself when you're feeling ashamed.

Instead Of	Try
I THOUGHT I'D BE FURTHER ALONG IN MY CAREER	I'VE ALREADY LEARNED SO MUCH.
I AM SUCH A LOSER	IT'S BEEN HARDER THAN I THOUGHT, BUT I'M STILL TRYING AND THAT'S WHAT MATTERS.
I CAN'T BELIEVE I DIDN'T GET THAT JOB	THAT WAS NOT THE JOB FOR ME. MY JOB IS STILL OUT THERE WAITING.
I'M TERRIBLE AT THIS	MOST PEOPLE STRUGGLE AT FIRST. COMMITTING TO LEARNING NEW SKILLS WILL HELP ME GROW.

RELATIONSHIPS MATTER

Even in our ever-isolated, online-driven, increasingly VR world, IRL relationships matter. When it comes to your ability to make successful Power Moves, your personal and professional relationships are absolutely critical. Knowing that getting along with other humans is important to your success seems like a no-brainer, right? Like, you *know* this, I *know* this, but even so, most of us struggle to prioritize strong, healthy, supportive connections with the people in our work world. And it's all understandable, really!

You get so distracted with meeting goals and deadlines, with keeping up your online brand, with clearing out your Netflix queue. We're all so exhausted at the end of these long, overstimulated days—with balancing full-time work and side hustles, with just keeping up the *basics of adulting*, tamping down anxiety, managing depression, just *staying afloat*—that many of us forget to call our moms and maintain even our most inner-circle friendships, let alone seek out and keep up with quality professional peers.

But research shows that—beyond career satisfaction—what actually makes us happiest is healthy, consistent, long-term relationships with the people around us (the inverse is true as well: toxic interactions with others can seriously negatively impact our daily happiness and even life expectancy).

When we invest in high-quality, positive relationships with coworkers or those in our professional orbit, when these relationships are grounded in respect, cooperation, and trust, we become better workers, more open to feedback and more engaged in our day-to-day tasks, no matter how mundane. Put another way: being close to coworkers makes work more fun.

Our connections to other people are also a strong indicator of our contentment level at work. In fact, those we choose to include in our networks will have a greater impact on how we think about ourselves and our position in life than almost anything else. A 2008 study out of Harvard University and the University of San Diego discovered that positive friends (or professional connections) will have a greater influence on our life satisfaction than external factors, like the amount of money we make.

So, as you are building out your professional résumé, make it a priority to build out and maintain a network of positive, supportive people whom you trust and can rely on, whose company makes you feel inspired. Not everyone will be your best friend, obviously, but thinking about the professional relationships in your life, how you cultivate them, how you network, and whom you let in is as important to your success as any other career strategy we've discussed. Ultimately, because it's human, connected, and real, putting time into this area of your life will be more rewarding than the other stuff too.

CHAPTER 12

Your Personal "Circle of Champions"

You've probably heard the adage: "You're the average of the five people you spend the most time with," right? Motivational speaker Jim Rohn's line about community and how our social networks influence our lives is so well-known it borders on cliché. But clichés become clichés for a reason—they're usually *true*, and therefore they resonate deeply. Rohn imagined that our closest friends and colleagues create a sphere of influence around us that, to some degree, dictates how we behave and how we think—if the people in your life are smokers, you will probably smoke too; if they spend Sundays watching *Vanderpump Rules* marathons and only taking breaks for Seamless orders, chances are you're going to join them; and if they are negative self-saboteurs, it's likely you will become one as well.

According to Harvard researcher and psychologist Dr. David McClelland, the people closest to you determine as much as 95 percent of your success or failure in life. (So, while we're talking clichés, I'll throw out another one: "Show me your friends and I'll show you your future," origin unknown, though my best guess is this originated on Pinterest.)

In all seriousness, Rohn's adage and McClelland's research are both predictive and cautionary and lay out clearly that the five people you spend the most time with—and specifically their day-to-day behaviors and deeply held beliefs—will shape who you are and how you spend your life. So, while you may have many people in both your virtual and real lives, the handful who are closest to you will most influence the choices you make, the goals you set, and how you move through the world.

I like to think of these five people (or more! You can have as many as you want!) as a personal "Circle of Champions." The people whom I know I can trust to guide me and whom I respect and believe in enough to invest my time in supporting their career journeys too.

A Circle of Champions is not networking (which we'll get to in a second), though some of your members may start out that way. A Circle of Champions is small and handpicked, carefully curated and chosen according to specific criteria, namely because they are people you admire, whose values, ambition, work ethic, and vision of success are aligned with your own. They are people who inspire you, your real-life sheroes, those you want to champion loudly and publicly over the long haul. They are people who expand your outlook and help you change course when needed. They are people you can trust and be open and honest and vulnerable with; people who will not abuse your openness, vulnerability, or trust.

It may seem harsh or cold to think about actual humans this way, as a calculus for success. But real talk: *Your friends are your future.* And you are theirs. And if you want to be in the driver's seat of your career and your life, not just a passenger watching it all float by, then there's nothing wrong with being intentional and proactive about how and with whom you spend your time.

So, what are the criteria for your Circle of Champions? this is obviously personal—only you know for sure both what y need and want, and what you offer—but here are some things to keep in mind.

Like anything else in your life, the people you choose to spend time with and the reasons you like spending time with them are subject to change. This is normal and healthy! Fighting it or holding on to relationships that make you feel bad is not. The professional friendships you form at an early age, when you're just starting out, may not serve you as you grow up and into your career. As you get older, experience new things, and evolve and grow, your goals and even your outlook on work will most likely change. It's okay to let people in your life go, or to see them less frequently when you're no longer aligned.

Instead of dwelling on how sad this can be (and yes, it is totally sad when you grow apart from someone or someone lets you down), remember that negativity, loneliness, demotivation, and even depression can be contagious, that you have to put yourself, your path, and your health first. Don't slam any doors shut—you don't have to be reactive or get pulled into any kinds of drama like big blown-out arguments, extreme emotions, anger, or shame—but just move thoughtfully, carefully through creating and cultivating a professional circle that suits your needs and wants right now.

Look around at the people you spend the most time with and ask yourself honestly: Are these relationships best aligned with who I am, who I want to be, and my vision of where I want to take my life? Are there people in my orbit whom I'd like to spend more time with, but I can't because my time is taken up by some who are not good to me? After you've asked and answered these questions, consider the following exercise.

Qualities of a High-Value Circle	Qualities of People You May Want to Ditch
ACTIONS ALIGN WITH VALUES	ACTIONS CONSISTENTLY CONTRADICT VALUES
HONEST, FORTHRIGHT	WITHHOLDING, SLIPPERY
CONSISTENT, SHOWS UP	FLAKES, CAN'T BE COUNTED ON
UNAFRAID TO DISAGREE, CHALLENGE OTHERS' BELIEF SYSTEMS	YES WOMEN, ALWAYS AGREE WITH ANYTHING YOU SAY
LISTENS	IS ALWAYS WAITING FOR THEIR TURN IN CONVERSATION
HAS FIRM, QUALITY BOUNDARIES	OVERSTEPS BOUNDARIES
CENTERS YOU AND YOUR EXPERIENCE WHEN YOU NEED THEM TO	CENTERS THEMSELVES ALWAYS
PRODUCES QUALITY WORK YOU ADMIRE	IS ALWAYS LOOKING FOR THE SCAM
RETAINS A MOSTLY HOPEFUL, POSITIVE OUTLOOK	CONSISTENTLY NEGATIVE, COMPLAINING, DOOMSDAY
IS DISCREET AND LOYAL, WILL HOLD YOUR SECRETS	USES PRIVATE/PERSONAL INFORMATION AS CURRENCY TO GET AHEAD
GENEROUS WITH TIME, OPPORTUNITIES	HOARDS WORK, IS SECRETIVE ABOUT PROJECTS
CHAMPIONS YOU AND YOUR SUCCESSES	DOESN'T HAVE TIME FOR, IS INDIFFERENT TO, YOUR SUCCESS

Audit Your Current Circle of Champions

It's your job to hire, fire, and promote accordingly in your own life.

1. **Surround yourself with optimists:** You now know that you'll essentially become the people whom you spend your time around the most. Are the people around you largely optimists or pessimists? If it's the latter, then try instead to align yourself with people who have a sunnier outlook. Their energy will be contagious!

2. **Surround yourself with people who challenge you:** People who agree with you all the time can keep you stagnating as much as anything else. Don't be afraid to seek out the strong-willed, the devil's advocates, the people who will (respectfully) offer a contrasting point of view. Learn to get comfortable in the discomfort of being challenged—don't run from it, don't get defensive, look at it as the gift it is and examine what it can teach you.

3. **Check yourself:** Are you showing up correctly for others? Are you making the time to invest in people you respect, not only when it's convenient for you but also when it's not? Are you a person people can count on? Are you negative more often than not? Do you champion others' successes? Have you cultivated good listening skills? Are you consistent? Optimism can be learned and good habits can be committed to—make sure you are showing up for others the way you'd like them to show up for you.

With time and experience, we learn just how important a role the people closest to us play in our lives and careers. Remember, your Circle of Champions is not a spontaneous networking group. They are an intentional group of people chosen because your values and visions of success are aligned. They don't compete with you or feel the need to one-up you. They are people you can share your future with, and while they may reply back with tough questions, those questions are rooted in respect and the joy to see you succeed. Practice regular audits with your current Circle of Champions and learn to thoughtfully let go of those with whom you no longer share compatibility. These moves will help you move forward with other parts of your career (and life) as well!

CHAPTER 13

The New Rules for Networking

One of the topics that comes up again and again at Career Contessa, one of the things our readers ask about more than anything else, is networking. Where do I begin finding my network? How do I build my network? How can I overcome anxiety about networking? What do I do if I hate the word *networking*?

The biggest mistake people usually make about networking is, instead of imagining it as relational and human-based (and therefore feeling-based), they treat their network like a twenty-four-hour ATM, ever ready for the next withdrawal. In reality, networking is not one-sided and, sticking with the ATM analogy, requires you to make deposits to your network before you can ever withdraw. It's two-way collaboration; it's an interconnected web of connections, of good feelings and best intentions that will expand and evolve, and that you can tap into and give back to over the course of your career. In fact, research shows that thinking of networking as a renewable resource to which you can give frequently and generously may very well set you up for greater success in the long term.

In his book *Give and Take*, award-winning researcher and social scientist Adam Grant discovered that, while the world is made of "givers" (those who put others' interests ahead of their own), "matchers" (those who aim to trade evenly), and "takers" (those who attempt to use others to maximize their own success), it's ultimately the givers who succeed most often and enjoy the most career success.

Givers tend to share their networks and business contacts and give time to mentoring and helping the careers of others. Givers are rare in that they contribute to others without expecting anything in return. Grant's research found that because modern success is increasingly dependent on how we interact with others—and because givers seek a relational way of working—givers tend to hold the highest positions on the org chart.

And, while traditional networking might feel slightly shallow—acquaintances, small talk, niceties: something that appears to only be transactional or without real, meaningful, personal reward—what we're really talking about here is *non*networking, which is building and maintaining genuine (or real!) connections and relationships. Plus, according to PayScale, 85 percent of open positions are found through networking. This means your time is very well spent when you're using it to build these real connections. After six years of research, advising, and trial and error at Career Contessa (along with my own career-long experiences in different networks), here is my best advice on how to get nonnetworking right.

Network Early—and Often

Here is the problem: you need something—a recommendation, a warm, informal introduction to a person at a certain company, etc.—and it is only at this time do you start thinking about your network, checking in, reaching out, contacting the people who you think can help. This is more of treating a network like an ATM! It's also among the biggest mistakes you can make. Because you have not kept up with the people in your network, because you're only showing up when you need something, you seem like a taker. And everyone (or at least most people) hates a taker. Show up earlier and build connections based on mutual respect and shared interests—not only what you can get out of them.

Break the Networking "Rules"

One of the best things you can do in networking is stand out—in a good way. So get creative about how you network, where you find the right contact, and how you reach out. For example: one unique networking idea when you're trying to build new relationships is to start an industry blog or podcast—make a dream networking list of everyone you'd love to be connected with, and even if it's one hundred people, ask them all. Odds are ten of them will say yes to a fifteen-minute interview. Your one hundred dream people should not just sit in the C-suite or be at the top of their careers; look for peers you respect at companies you admire. People love talking about their careers—and even if your blog or podcast has an audience of twenty, you're getting your most important questions answered, giving that audience of twenty something valuable, and making new connections all at once.

Other ideas include starting a book club where each person invites one new friend each month or joining/starting an IRL Quilt chat with the networking app Quilt. If you're a woman who's also a mom, check out the Peanut app. Maybe you'd like to send a more thoughtful outreach via a gift to a potential client. Try BoxFox for gifting and pick something that's small yet personalized to stand out. The point here is to get creative with how you network, and once you've developed a relationship, make sure you stay in touch on a regular basis. Maintaining your network matters (almost) more than creating a network, but more on that in a bit.

Know Your Networking Objective

Networking events can be intense, and most people would not (and do not) attend them without some kind of mission. If you don't have an answer to "What do I want?" or "Why am I here?" you probably don't need to be at this particular networking event just yet. Before you attend, consider: What will your objective or learning goal be? Meeting potential employers? Finding a new client for your business? Learning from successful entrepreneurs in your field? Meeting people in a similar industry who are your peers? Is there a specific person you want to get in front of and meet? Are you there to support the company? Any reason works but you need to have *something*. Decide now, write it down, and don't allow yourself to leave the event until you've accomplished your mission.

Find Events (and People) That Best Meet Your Goals

Now that you know what your objective is, find the events that best suit it. Check out the hosts, the speakers, and the topics being covered. If it's something you're already an expert on, look for a more advanced session. These are skill-specific opportunities for you to advance your career through developing and honing in on your strengths—or, hey, your weaknesses.

Be mindful about choosing an event style that will give you a chance to shine in our networking-cluttered world. Because the options are vast, you can—and should—network in a way that will suit your needs and where you can bring your A-game. If you *hate* icebreakers and small talk—maybe a roundtable isn't for you. Maybe you prefer to listen to panelists and then break into small groups to workshop specific skills. Maybe a specific class where you're learning and applying a skill works best. Maybe you prefer informational interviews over coffee or the phone because one-on-one networking is more comfortable for you. When I was trying to transition from an administrative assistant to a recruiter, I did it through informational interviews with female recruiters in the LA area.

Regardless of where and when you're meeting the person, make sure to collect their information—specifically, their email, if you can. Maybe they have a business card, or maybe they're willing to just share their email directly. Write it down (notes on your phone work too!) and then add a note or two about what you discussed. You can also consider creating a networking tracker in a basic Excel spreadsheet or Google Doc that helps you stay organized on whom you met, where and when, what you discussed, and any next steps. Personalized information will be important for our next networking tip to help you stand out.

Follow Up—Quickly—After You Meet

The first twenty-four hours after meeting a new person are the most important because this is the first step to building a genuine connection—and you're still fresh in the person's mind from yesterday. After you meet the person, whether virtually or in person, whether at a large event or small workshop, send them an email and include something personal that you two discussed. Here's an example:

> *Hi Name,*
>
> *It was really great to meet you at last night's Ladies in Tech event. I especially enjoyed your advice on how to ask your boss to work on the projects that align with your skills. I plan to follow your suggested steps and will let you know how it goes!*
> *In the meantime, I'd love to stay in touch and connect on LinkedIn. Please let me know if there's anything I can do to help support you.*
>
> *Best,*
> *Name*

Adding a personal anecdote is a great way to stand out in the sea of networking emails. Unless the two of you discussed a specific ask, your follow-up email doesn't have to extend past a "Nice to meet you, and I loved chatting to you about XYZ." As you close your email, be sure to ask them if it's okay for you to add them as a connection on LinkedIn, and then you can sign off with "I look forward to staying in touch." Or, even better— "I look forward to staying in touch, and please let me know if I can help you at all." Offering to give is key, and so is a timely follow-up.

Really Maintain Your Relationships

After the initial follow-up comes maintaining. Something I see all the time is network neglect. This means that at some point you took the time to build your network by having an objective and getting in front of the right people, you sent that post-event "nice to meet you" follow-up, and then . . . crickets. When I ask people why they let the relationship drop off there, they often reply with "I didn't have anything else to talk to them about."

True networking is about relationship building, and you can't build if you've only followed up with the person once. At a minimum, ask to add the person as a connection on LinkedIn, which will allow you to stay somewhat up-to-date on any major career changes they make. This means commenting on their work anniversary, sharing news that's relevant to them, congratulating them when you see their company in the news, etc. But even better? The seasonal email outreach. I do this twice a year after New Year's and the Fourth of July with a simple message like this:

Dear Name,

I hope you had a wonderful (insert holiday). My family and I (insert how you spent your holiday). I'm reaching out to touch base with you and give you a quick update on what's happening in my world.

(Insert any update—this could be with your career, side hustle, personal list, etc. Tell them what you've accomplished lately or what you're focused on for the future.) I look forward to staying in touch and please let me know if there's anything

*I can do to support you. Until then, I'll keep up with you on
LinkedIn.*

Best,
Name

This is one of the easiest ways to stay top of mind with your
network, and it makes it way more comfortable to reach out with
an ask if/when you need it in the future.

Respect the Double Opt-In

So, you've got a network that you're consistently building and
maintaining with genuine outreach—wonderful! Now comes
your colleague/BFF/mom/new person you met, and you think an
introduction between your friend and someone in your network
would be mutually beneficial for them both, so you offer to connect your friend. HOLD UP. Before you send your email to introduce these two people, we should discuss the double opt-in. This
means that both people opt in to being introduced via email *first*.
Yes, it's a bit more effort on your part to ask your network first if
you can make the introduction, but people REALLY appreciate
when they: 1) have their time respected and 2) get a heads-up.
Maybe they are in the middle of a project and it's not a good time.
Maybe they just don't want to be introduced. Whatever their reason, the double opt-in allows them to do what works for them
without you adding a new assignment to their plate—sending a
decline email to your friend. Plus, if they are open to the connection, it will probably be more successful. Here's an example of
what you might send:

Hi Name,

Congratulations on your work anniversary! LinkedIn updates are super helpful, and when I saw that you're now working in business development, I immediately thought of my friend Mallory, who's trying to transition into that field.

   Mallory has a similar background to yours, and she's looking to connect with other like-minded women on how they made their own transitions. Would it be okay if I introduced you two via email so she can set up an informational interview with you?

Best,
Name

Don't Be Afraid to Ask for Connections

Yes, it's important to respect the double opt-in, but I don't want this extra step to intimidate anyone from asking their network for help—or telling someone, "No, I'd rather not be connected right now." I was talking to a friend the other day who wanted to email a past coworker but didn't. When I asked her why not, she told me, "Well, I feel bad annoying her."

Ladies, can we please stop feeling bad asking for what we want? Can we ditch the people-pleasing and the quest to be liked by everyone? Not only will it help aid your mental and emotional health efforts, it's also a waste of time to worry about the other person liking/not liking you because you asked for their help. If you asked for their help in a respectful way, are making as many networking "deposits" as you are "withdrawals," and have crafted a clear, concise email, what's holding you back?

Consider the worst-case scenario (like you don't receive an email reply back) and the real reason for your fear of annoying them/not being liked. Remember, when a preoccupation with likability butts heads with your ideas, your goals, or your vision, it's simply not worth it. It's in recognizing these crucial moments that you must do away with likability—and send the damn email.

Compose a Networking Email That Will Actually Get Opened

Outside of your "warm contacts" (e.g., people you met at an event, were introduced to, etc.), there will be people you want to network with that you've never met. These are "cold" connections, and your outreach will probably start with a cold email. No one likes sending a cold email—it can be intimidating, anxiety-producing, and awkward as hell. But once you demystify the process and understand exactly how to do it, you might even learn to like it. Here's what I've found works well:

1. **Define your learning goal:** When crafting your cold email, keep things concise, professional, and easy. The goal is to communicate your message with as little back-and-forth as possible. Before you sit down to write, you should start by asking yourself what your learning goal is with this email (are you starting to sense a theme with networking?!). What you write depends on what you want. Maybe you want to change industries or

meet up with someone to see what their work is really like. Or you're looking to get involved with an organization in your community but would like to know more first. Be clear about your goal.

2. **Create a "connection":** People are pressed for time. The person you're reaching out to will be more likely to help you out if you share common interests or experiences. Did you both attend the same university for undergrad? Do you have a friend or a previous employer in common? Are you interested in their career path or company? Did you attend an event they were a speaker at? Mention it in your email.

3. **Craft your email:** Once you figure out whom you want to email and what you'd like from them, it's time to format that email.

- Start by introducing yourself, telling the person what you do.
- Note your common acquaintance(s) or shared interest.
- Clearly outline how you think they can help you.
- Include a direct ask, specifically a call to action. Your job is to make it easy for them to say yes to your request, so stay away from asking them to give you an hour of their time for after-work drinks. Instead, ask for a twenty-minute phone call with specifics about what you want to cover. Is it their career path, company, advice on entrepreneurship? Remember that you can start with a quick, convenient phone call and then work your way up to a happy-hour invite!
- If you're looking to schedule a time to talk to them, make sure to be generous with your availability—you're asking them for a favor! I also prefer when people include their availability in the initial email outreach, but stay away from sharing a link to

your calendar tool, because that can irritate people. A better way to offer your availability would be with something like, "I'm free after four p.m. every Monday to Friday."

4. **Use an effective cold email subject line:** What you put in your subject line can make all the difference. Here are some ideas.

- If you're lucky and already have a common connection, try this: "Anna, Mark Johnson recommended I reach out."
- If you don't know them but found and read some of their published work, try this: "Ms. Connor, I loved your LinkedIn article on networking."
- If you don't have much to go on at all, offer value: "Social Media Manager with Nonprofit Expertise Interested in Helping Your Team."
- When all else fails, try a question: "Any advice for someone who loves the marketing work you're doing at Company X?"

Keep Your Expectations Realistic

Once you've sent your email, it's time to be patient and wait it out. Don't hound the person until they respond to you. Give them a two-week window to respond before you write a follow-up email. If you haven't heard from them in that span of time, follow up in a reply to your previous email so that they see both messages in the same thread. If they don't respond after your follow-up, you may want to move on to someone in a similar position and see if they'd be interested in helping you out. This is especially important if you've been trying to get in touch with a senior-level employee. Elise Loehnen, the chief content officer at Goop, echoed this idea by recommending that people consider horizontal networking if they're not hearing back. Horizontal networking is just a fancy way of saying that you'll try to network with the people who sit "beside" you as peers. And if the person does get back to you but says they need you to circle back to them in a few months—do it! Add it to your calendar so you don't forget. Don't be discouraged by the lack of response—when I was researching how to transition from administrative assistant to recruiter, I reached out to seventy-plus recruiters for informational interviews on LinkedIn over nine months, and only thirty of them got back to me. I had less than a 50 percent response rate, but I didn't let that stop me from trying, and neither should you!

If you do meet with them to talk about their employer or industry, please don't show up expecting that this meeting is going to get you a job. Be honest with them and yourself about your expectations. If you really want to get the inside scoop on PR and marketing for a nonprofit, then show up only expecting to have a conversation and learn something. Come prepared with great questions that you can't already find the answers to on the internet a million times. Or tailor your questions based on your research, like "I noticed you worked in advertising before you switched to tech. Why did you make that transition?" Assuming you find no other information about the person or you want ideas to help you ask great questions that you can then tailor, here are some to consider:

- Can you tell me a bit about your career path and what led you to the role you're in today?

- What were some of your early roles in the field?
- What does a workday look like for you?
- What are some big projects you're working on now or that you've finished up in the last few months?
- What do you enjoy most about the work you do? / What are you most excited about right now?
- What do you enjoy the least? Or, is there something that surprised you about the role when you first started?
- What skills do you think are most important for someone interested in a job like yours?
- Do you think there's a personality type that's not well suited for this kind of career?
- What are some of the biggest challenges you face day-to-day?
- What about the biggest rewards?
- What do you wish you'd known when you were starting out in this career?
- Where do you see yourself in five or ten years?
- Do you have any recommendations for other people I should talk to or other resources I should explore?
- Are there any questions I'm not asking that I should be?
- Would it be all right for us to stay in touch?

It's very impressive to have a networking conversation with someone who has done their homework, asks great questions, and stays in touch. If anything more comes out of it, that'll just be a bonus. And these bonuses *do* happen. When I left my job at Hulu, my replacement was a woman who had reached out for a horizontal networking conversation about eight months earlier. While the role wasn't open at that time, we had a great conversation and she stayed in touch, so when Hulu asked for referrals, I immediately thought of her. That's how cold networking can and does turn into new opportunities.

Don't Forget to Follow Through

If the person agrees to meet up with you or answer some questions via email, be courteous, punctual, and respectful of their time. There's no shame in getting right down to business when you finally meet; in fact, the person on the other side will probably really appreciate it, and you should always be the one to direct the conversation. Remember—you want to make this easy on them and impress them with your preparedness. You should treat it the same as you would a job interview, whether the purpose of the conversation is personal or professional. And be sure to follow up within twenty-four hours to thank them for their time.

Turning Networking into Long-Term Mentorship

Networking meetups and/or informational interviews don't necessarily have to end at the coffee shop door or as LinkedIn connections. If you're inspired by someone or feel you have real chemistry, it's perfectly acceptable to respectfully attempt to cultivate a mentor-mentee relationship. After your initial meeting, and after the follow-up thank-you and niceties, check back in. Tell the person how their career or outlook inspires you and even what actions you took because of their advice. If you're comfortable, ask directly if they'd have time to be in contact once a month, if you can schedule regular time to meet—even a twenty-minute FaceTime or call. Stay in touch when you have news, want their input/advice, or have something you feel could be relevant or helpful to your potential mentor.

If being in touch on a regular basis doesn't fit their schedule, you still have the seasonal email outreach we covered earlier in this tool. Always, always be polite and respectful of busy schedules, and keep your meetings concise and direct. Follow their lead with communication (do they prefer email? Text? Slack?), maintain proper boundaries (don't, for example, send them texts at midnight), and keep a respectful digital distance by avoiding overengaging on social platforms, sliding into their DMs, or becoming demanding of their time.

Paying Networking Forward

If we follow Grant's theory of givers and takers, giving more (when it's reasonable and you can do it without overextending yourself or depleting your own personal reserves) is the ticket to creating the success and professional fulfillment we're all searching for. And also, it makes you feel good. Prioritizing giving back, being generous with advice, connections (as long as you're mindful of the double-opt-in rule!), and mentorship actually helps build relationships with people you like and respect and often leads to lifelong professional friendships.

Your career will ebb and flow, and there will be times when you feel professionally settled and stable and have more to give. Capitalize on these moments and build time into your weekly or monthly schedule for mentorship and connecting people in your network. Call it karma or whatever you like, but investing in giving when you can will pay dividends in the future—when you do

finally have a need or an ask (and you will! We all do!), you'll
have built up a reserve of goodwill with people who are more than
happy and even enthusiastic about helping you.

Don't Flake—Actually Show Up

The simplest step is sometimes the hardest. In order to conquer
your fear of networking, you need to actually show up at the event.
In economics and game theory, there's something called a "commitment device." In essence, it's something you do *now* to keep
yourself honest or committed to an action you already know your
future self will not be excited about. It's why people buy expensive gym memberships (to avoid slacking off on workouts) or buy
expensive healthy groceries on Sundays (to avoid slacking off on
their homemade work lunches).

For networking purposes, you'll use two simple commitment
devices to get yourself there:

1. You're going to prepay for a ticket (assuming the event you're
   attending has a fee).
2. You're going to tell someone you're going.

Once the money has been spent and the announcement made,
you will be significantly less likely to let yourself hang back simply
because you just don't "feel like it." And speaking of Networking
Don'ts, some others are below.

Another critical piece of showing up in networking is persistence, following up regularly and often; even if you hear nothing back, even if it makes you want to die—persistence works. I'm
living proof that you can change your career with persistence.

Networking Don'ts

DON'T BE TOO THIRSTY IN PERSON	DON'T STALK PEOPLE ONLINE	DON'T SLIDE INTO DMS ON MORE THAN ONE PLATFORM
BE AWARE OF SOMEONE'S TIME AND GAUGE THEIR INTEREST IN YOUR EXCHANGE.	RESPECT BOUNDARIES AND LEARN TO TAKE A HINT, IF SOMEONE DOESN'T RESPOND AFTER TWO ATTEMPTS AT CONTACT (THREE IF IT'S A CRITICAL CONNECTION) LET IT DROP.	MOST PROFESSIONALS WILL NOT TAKE KINDLY TO SIMULTANEOUS INSTA, TWITTER, LINKEDIN, AND FACEBOOK CHATS SO MAKE SURE TO SLOW YOUR ROLL A BIT.
DON'T SHOW UP UNPREPARED	DON'T MAKE IT ALL ABOUT YOU	DON'T FORGET TO FOLLOW UP
DO YOUR HOMEWORK ON POTENTIAL CONNECTIONS, KNOW AT LEAST A FEW FACTS ABOUT THEIR CAREERS, WHY YOU THINK THEY'RE COMPELLING.	SHOW GENUINE INTEREST IN THE PEOPLE YOU'RE MEETING AND ENGAGING WITH, GET TO KNOW THEM A BIT, DON'T PUSH A NETWORKING AGENDA STRAIGHT OFF.	CRITICAL STEP. TOO OFTEN A PERSON WILL GO THROUGH ALL OF THE TROUBLE OF NETWORKING, MEET INTERESTING PEOPLE AND THEN NEVER EVER FOLLOW UP.

Those thirty informational interviews laid the groundwork for me to learn about recruiting careers and narrow in on what type of recruiter I wanted to be and the work environment that would suit my values. When I interviewed at Hulu, I was up against people with real recruiting experience, but I stood out because my ability to connect the dots between my passion for the role/company and how to bring value to their organization was BEYOND the typical "I've done this job already, and I can do it again" explanation. Experience matters, but don't get hung up on the notion that only previous "official" work experience counts.

CHAPTER 14

The Art of Saying No

If telling someone no is hard and uncomfortable for you, you're not alone. Part of the reason why you might feel conflicted about saying no is because you're *actually* free. This means you haven't already committed to something else in your schedule. However, that doesn't mean you want to or should say yes to what's being asked of you. This happens to me a lot because I do suffer from FOND: Fear of Not Doing. Essentially, this feeling is what happens when you feel guilty for spending free moments of your time not being "productive." For example, binge-watching Bravo versus attending a networking event, taking time to work on your side hustle, etc.

While I'm actively working to shift my attitude, I *do* feel guilty for spending free moments just being free, which pushes me to say yes to things big, small, urgent, nonurgent, and everything in between. However, I've learned the hard way that if you are saying yes to a lot of small things, then they keep you too busy to say yes to the important stuff—like the Power Moves you want to make.

So how can you filter when to say no or yes? First, ask yourself if the opportunity is aligned with your goals or vision for how you want to spend your time. Does this "thing" being asked of you get you closer or further?

Figuring out what you need to be saying no to is challenging, not only because you don't want to disappoint people but also because people tend to have a warped perspective of time. This warped perspective, called "planning fallacy," first proposed by Daniel Kahneman and Amos Tversky in 1979, is a phenomenon in which predictions about how much time will be needed to complete a future task display an optimism bias and underestimate the time needed. Therefore, the further something is in the future, the more time we think we have. For example, if it's January and someone asks you about doing something in June, it's so far away, your schedule is wide open, and so you (incorrectly) feel like the normal issues you typically struggle with in terms of how busy you are and how much you have on your plate won't apply at all in June, so you say yes.

This pattern can *and* will repeat itself unless you change your behavior. To help combat filling your plate with busy "yes" items, Laura Vanderkam, a time management expert, recommends the following:

1. **When you're asked to do something in the future, ask yourself if you would do it tomorrow:** That's because your sense of how busy you will be tomorrow is far better that your sense for something far ahead in the future. When asked about getting coffee with someone in two weeks, consider if you'd get coffee with them tomorrow. If the answer is no, then that's probably how you'll feel two weeks from now as well.

2. **Train yourself to recognize which things align with your vision and which things are just keeping you busy:** Consider your opportunities on a zero-to-ten-point scale—you might be better off saying no to things that are in the middle because it is quite possible that good stuff will come up later that is in the nine or ten category. For example, if you booked up most of your June schedule and then this amazing opportunity comes your way when your employer wants to fly you to Paris to attend a conference with your boss, you'd either have to get out of the little stuff or miss the trip to Paris. Do you really want to be known as the girl who didn't go to Paris?! *[Pro tip: not going to Paris worked out for Lauren Conrad, but (overall) the answer to this is a resounding no!]*

So when people ask you to do time-specific stuff that is far in the future, it needs to be big enough to justify a yes. If it is something you want to do, Vanderkam recommends you tell people, "I can do it for you next week, but I can't pledge to do it in June." That's recognizing the opportunity cost is important as well.

CHAPTER 15

Relationships Outside of Work

Networking is important, career mentors and cheerleaders have immense value, and work friends (including work husbands and wives) can feel like literal lifelines as you plow through your eight-hour-plus days. But what about your world outside of your job? Deprioritizing friends and family, being "always on" professionally, and making yourself accessible to coworkers around the clock are all signs of a work/life imbalance and just a bummer-problem relationship with your career, which can impact those you love.

When it comes to making successful Power Moves, your relationships outside of work are an essential source of support. And trust me, this is something that can be invaluable and make all the difference. The unconditional support is how you're able to endure challenges, cope with the unknown, and maintain some sense of balance between work and life.

Setting boundaries around work so you can enjoy the humans in your life is critical. But equally as significant is investing time in communication, in having an open dialogue with the people closest to you and setting realistic, agreed-upon expectations so everyone understands the big career decisions you'll likely have to make (like a potential relocation for a job) and the small daily-grind ones (needing to work on the weekend, being late for a dinner).

If it's a life partner you're talking to, these decisions should be discussed as far in advance as possible, and mutual goal setting should be a frequent and shared event. Compromise will always be necessary, but each person in the relationship should have their opinion heard, and attempts at sincere collaboration should be made. The ability to endure these difficult conversations, show up with respect and kindness, be as honest as you can about your needs, listen openly to theirs, learn how to share responsibilities, and find shared ground when you can—all of this will become the difference between a satisfying partnership and one that's fueled by grievances and resentments.

Take the time to talk to your partner, to share your big wild dreams and your more realistic, tidy aspirations. Adulthood and families of all kinds are complicated, and no one's needs will be met at all times, but talking it out, having it all on the table in healthy, productive ways, will help you share the victories and shoulder the inevitable storms ahead.

Here are some other tricks to maintaining nonwork relationships:

1. **Have at least one day a week when you're completely "off":** No Slack, no email checking, no "let me just finish up this one thing." Alert your coworkers ahead of time: "I will be checking out completely on Saturdays" and put an out-of-office message on your email so no one is expecting a response. Alert your friends and family that this time is for them.
2. **Stop multitasking:** Even if you're not technically "off" for the day, when you've committed your time to another person—a

child, a partner, your mom—make a vow to be present. Don't check your email during dinner, don't just send a few reminders between your kid's bath time and bed. Give the people you love your full attention. Work *can* wait.

3. **Plan nonwork fun:** One of the reasons all of our time gets sucked up by work is because it's an easy distraction, and there's always something more you can probably do. A pattern I see with myself is when I'm trying to think of what to do with my free time, I will grab my laptop to find a hike or order some stuff for my house and—BAM!—the next thing I know I've gone down a work rabbit hole and given most of my weekend over to work. Instead of falling into this trap, try:

   • Prioritize planning weekend activities—game nights, dinners out, dinners in, drinks at a new bar you've been dying to try, a performance, an afternoon hike. Planning makes the people in your life feel important and like you want to invest your time in them, like you care.
   • Organize weekend trips away—visit friends in faraway cities or meet in a mutually agreed-upon place. Travel and a change of scenery is bonding and will make you head into work on Monday refreshed, with a new perspective and point of view.

4. **Actively cultivate relationships outside of work:** Spend as much time as you can with friends and family members who don't work with you. If you have friends who are also coworkers, set a rule that you won't talk about work outside of work. Try to stick to it! When meeting new people, a great way to keep your conversation away from work and more focused on other parts of your life (like family, hobbies, etc.) is to not ask them what they do unless it comes up naturally in conversation. Think about it:

asking someone what they do is usually the first or second question you ask after just meeting them. Right away that turns your nonwork conversation toward work—and makes it challenging to ever have your identity rooted in who you are (versus your job title). This is a piece of advice I learned from Tess Vigeland, an author and veteran journalist whose own research found that starting a conversation around work was mostly an American trait. Instead, Vigeland recommends asking people what they do for fun, any upcoming travel plans, the last restaurant they enjoyed, etc.

You'll never regret the time you spend maintaining quality relationships outside of work. They're critical to how you approach almost everything you do—from your performance at work to how you navigate life in general. After all, the healthiest thing is to make sure work is just one piece of the pie—not the whole thing.

TAKE CONTROL
OF YOUR CAREER

All right, we're finally ready to tackle what could be a book on its own—how to take control of your career and become your own career coach. In movie terms, you'll be the producer, director, and lead actor. Now that you appreciate the importance of taking care of yourself (self-care) and developing the support of others (relationships), it's time to manage the career you want.

No matter where you are in your career, I imagine by now you've learned (possibly the hard way) that no one is going to understand and look out for your needs and interests and career progress with the same commitment (and obsession) as you. That shouldn't be a surprise, because no one cares about the outcome more than you do.

Fortunately, you are more than up for the challenge! From mastering communication skills at work to setting appropriate-to-you goals to teaching people how they can and cannot treat you, your career provides you with an opportunity to learn and stretch yourself in ways you might not otherwise do. Here are the key Power Move tools that will help you take charge and manage the career you want.

CHAPTER 16

Abandoning the Elusive "Dream Job"

Unfortunately, we're not strangers to this "landing the dream job didn't bring me satisfaction" story at Career Contessa. Recently, a reader shared with me that she's a thirty-something-year-old naturopathic doctor working in a private practice. It was her dream since eighth grade to have this job, and she worked tirelessly to get there with education, additional jobs, and more. Now that she has it, she's not fulfilled, it doesn't bring her joy at all, and she wants to figure out what *is* the career move for her. The catch? She first needs to break away from chasing a dream job in the first place.

Like I mentioned before, a dream job will not solve all of your challenges any more than a dream partner will. And in order to truly get what you want, you'll need to shift your thinking from what you think work "should look like" to defining how work should best work for *you*. To do this, you need to start exploring your own internal needs. Instead of looking for a job that "fills" the missing parts of your life, you need to explore ways to find work that supports your priorities, integrates with your life, and can evolve with you long-term. That's the *real* dream.

Defining "Dream Job" (and Why You Don't Actually Want It)

When you imagine your dream job, it's probably a tad fuzzy, more like the "concept" of work than actually working. In this land of professional make-believe, you've identified a career you are passionate about and landed a position that is a consistent source of happiness and fulfillment, where you get to live a balanced life while being valued, respected, rewarded, and more than well compensated for what you do. Sounds idyllic, right? I know how lovely that daydream is because I lived inside it for a long time, and why this concept matters so much is because you can spend a lot of time, energy, and mental space landing that dream job, only to discover something is still missing. Life is not a Monopoly game. There is no passing "go" and collecting two hundred dollars. If you pass "go" in real life and ditch the work required to build a career on your terms, you end up in an ambition ditch.

In a study from 2017, researchers at Stanford University found the myth of the dream job is closely aligned with the myth that human beings have "fixed" passions and that once we "find our passion" and apply it to work, we will be fulfilled. This philosophy suggests that, at a certain point, we stop developing areas of interest and that we won't need to expand and grow. It can be stifling and limiting to signify an endgame when many of us have just gotten started, and, perhaps worst of all, it can make us tired and reluctant to try new things. According to the Stanford study: "Urging people to find their passion may lead them to put all their eggs in one basket but then to drop that basket when it becomes difficult to carry."

So, spoiler alert: turns out the dream job is a gargantuan, intangible concept because . . . it doesn't really exist, nor would you want it to. While it may be tidy to think so, our dreams are never about just one destination—the best careers are circuitous, meandering, and a little bit wild.

They adapt to our changing work-life needs and keep us excited and engaged. The perfect job when you're in your twenties will most likely be totally different to you when you're in your thirties, forties, and beyond, which is a great thing!

To quote a woman I've long admired, Ellevest CEO Sallie Krawcheck from a February 2018 interview for Quartz at Work: "I wish I had known that that process of figuring out what you're good at, what you want to do, and where you want to have an impact is not a one-time exercise, but an ongoing one. Instead, I bought into success being an endpoint rather than a constant process. Your career is not going to go the way you planned. It is impossible at the age of 23 to pick the right industry, the right company, and you can visualize what you're going to be doing in your 40s, 50s, and 60s, but chances are that it's going to be something quite different. So, remain open to opportunities and change."

The best thing you can do to keep yourself unstuck is to ditch the dream job altogether.

What You Should be Doing (Instead of Dream Job Hunting)

All of this doesn't mean you can't find (or create) a job you love. Finding a job you love starts with you—and understanding what you really want and need. And by the way, understanding what you *really* want and need is not always what you first think.

To get started, we're going to make some lists. For many of us, the task of being asked to write lists is like asking a sugar addict trying to avoid cravings to attend the Museum of Ice Cream. We know you love making lists, but these are going to be different because they are far from your daily to-do list. And we need you to promise that you won't jump into the pool of sprinkles (ahem, to-do lists) and that's the last we ever hear from you. We need you to stay focused on these lists because they will build toward a major Power Move. And remember that these lists are based on how you feel right now—as your career interest and stage in life evolve, you can make new lists.

Creating some preliminary lists will help you turn this dream job paradigm on its tired head. These lists are the start of letting go of the idea of a "dream job" and allowing yourself to identify and seek work you need that fits into the life you want. We call these your career ideals. Let's break this down into some action-able lists, starting with identifying your career ideals or, in more simple terms, your wants and needs.

Identify What You Want

Desire is tricky, of course, as it tends to be myopic, materialist, and often unrealistic. "I want a brownstone in Brooklyn!" "I would like to vacation internationally each month and wear new designer clothes while I'm doing it!" "How about a summer home?!" "Ready for my in-home chef to arrive any day now!" When you're listing out what you "want," start small, try to stay away from the mate-rial for now, and zero in on the "nice-to-haves" that would elevate your day-to-day life and help you feel more content and satisfied. For example, nearly 70 percent of small businesses offer some sort of flex work time—which can take the form of remote work, off-the-grid scheduling/hours, unlimited time off, or time off for education or volunteering. If your company doesn't have this and it's something you want, you can start to explore companies that offer this kind of flexibility.

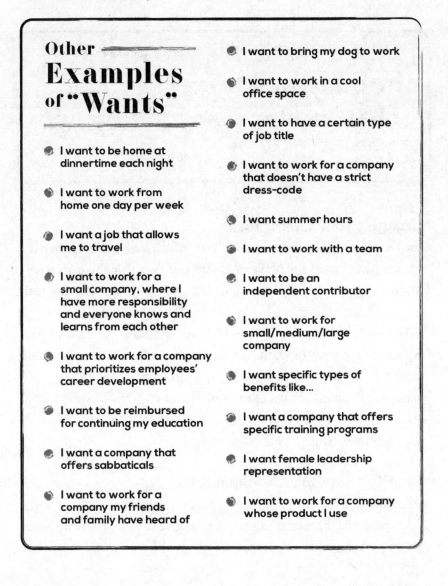

Other Examples of "Wants"

- I want to be home at dinnertime each night

- I want to work from home one day per week

- I want a job that allows me to travel

- I want to work for a small company, where I have more responsibility and everyone knows and learns from each other

- I want to work for a company that prioritizes employees' career development

- I want to be reimbursed for continuing my education

- I want a company that offers sabbaticals

- I want to work for a company my friends and family have heard of

- I want to bring my dog to work

- I want to work in a cool office space

- I want to have a certain type of job title

- I want to work for a company that doesn't have a strict dress-code

- I want summer hours

- I want to work with a team

- I want to be an independent contributor

- I want to work for small/medium/large company

- I want specific types of benefits like...

- I want a company that offers specific training programs

- I want female leadership representation

- I want to work for a company whose product I use

Identify Your Needs

Your needs differ from wants because they are nonnegotiable, fixed, your "must-haves." Are you a parent? A caretaker? The breadwinner of your family? Do you have special needs that your work must fulfill?

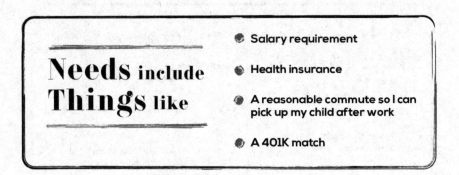

Needs include **Things** like

- Salary requirement
- Health insurance
- A reasonable commute so I can pick up my child after work
- A 401K match

Organize Your Career Ideals

Let's organize your career ideals and prioritize each by using the Career Ideals worksheet. For example, if you identified that you want to work with a team, you can get more specific on your Career Ideals worksheet by describing that you "need to have" at least one colleague but a "nice-to-have" would be a team of four or five. Maybe your "want" item is a team that works in-person together. By thinking through your wants and needs more, you'll better understand what's really important to you. As well, recognize that your career ideals will change throughout your life, so you can revisit this worksheet at any time.

Identify Your Target Companies

Now comes a fun part. You get to go on a scavenger hunt of sorts. Take your list of career ideals and shelve them for a bit while we explore companies where you might like to work—we'll call

Career Ideals

Let's identify your wants, needs, and nice-to-haves for all the categories that matter most to you. Get as specific as possible.

CATEGORY/ ITEM	NON-NEGOTIABLE I **NEED** THIS	I SEE IT I LIKE IT I **WANT** IT	THIS WOULD BE **NICE-TO-HAVE**
EX: Commute	30 mins. or less, one-way	Paid parking	Public transportations options

these target companies. For now, your list of companies should be broad—don't limit yourself. Your list might include websites you read often, products you love, industries you're obsessed with, services you're a longtime fan of, or even the company where your BFF works. Perhaps you're interested in companies that offer specific perks, ones you follow in the news or really admire because of their leadership team.

The goal is to create a long list of companies and be able to answer why each made the list with at least one sentence. And get creative by browsing additional sites like InHerSight, Glassdoor, Indeed, LinkedIn, Built In, and The Muse, while taking note of any companies you might want to learn more about. Add those to your Target Companies list.

Get to Know Your Target Companies

By now, you know what's important to have in your career. And you've also identified target companies. Now comes the part where we start to match companies to your career ideals, and this is where the (career) magic happens. We like to compare this to ordering a massive amount of clothes online, and now you'll be trying on each item/company to see if it fits. Only the target companies that match a majority of your career ideals should remain on your list. You might have to reprioritize your career ideals even more as you compare them to your target companies.

You can determine which companies stay—and which ones go—by using the Company Research worksheet for each company on your Target Companies list. You'll get to know the organizations much more extensively—and in way more detail than what you learn from a single job description. From there, you can cross off any target companies that are misaligned with your career ideals, which you might also adjust in this process.

Let's use an example to see how this works. You know your lifestyle isn't compatible with a lengthy commute. Given your additional research, you conclude that the hypothetical Acme

Target Companies

First, write down any and every company that interests you and why it made the list. Don't censor yourself. It's important to understand why you're interested in the company because you'll need to answer that in your resume, interview, etc.

TARGET COMPANY	WHY IT MADE THE LIST

Target Company

CAREER IDEAL	TARGET COMPANY	RESEARCH
MUST-HAVE A COMMUTE 30 MINS. OR LESS.	ACME COMPANY	30 MIN. COMMUTE BUT ONLY IF I CAN HAVE FLEX HOURS AND THEY DON'T OFFER FLEX HOURS.

Company requires a commute of at least thirty minutes each way, which of course is not suited to your needs unless they offer flexible work hours (which they don't). So, Acme Company ends up getting removed from your list of target companies.

Last, you can narrow down your list of target companies even further by asking yourself the following questions:

- Would working at this company require me to move/would I be willing to move?
- How does my experience align with the work this company does?
- What kind of work would I like to do for them?
- What experience or additional training do I need for this kind of role?
- Is there anyone in my network who can connect me to this company?
- Is there anyone with whom I could conduct an informational interview?

For companies that *are* aligned with you, it's time to start considering departments or roles that might be a good fit and focus your job search on just these specific companies. The more focused and specific your job search is, the more success you'll have with it. In recruiting we have a phrase called "spray and pray." This is when a candidate sprays their résumé all over the internet and prays that a recruiter will pick it up. They won't. Recruiters and companies are looking for candidates who can not only add value to the organization, solve challenges, collaborate with others, etc., but also clearly make a case for how their values and goals align with those of a target company. Value fitting is how you find a job you love, a genuine culture and role match that your ideal company clearly wants.

Company Research

For each company listed on your target companies list, you'll get to know the organizations way more extensively—and way more than what you read is a single job description by filling out one worksheet per company. From there you can cross off any target companies that are misaligned with your career ideals. And for companies that are aligned to you, it's time to start considering departments or roles you might be a good fit for and focusing your job search on just these specific companies. Job searches are more successful when you're focused on what company and job you want vs. applying to everything and anything. Think quality over quantity.

Company Name

If The Company Stays, Which Department or Role Will You Pursue:

WHAT YOU WANT TO KNOW	WHERE TO START YOUR SEARCH	NOTES AND RESEARCH	HOW DOES THIS COMPARE TO YOUR SPECIFIC CAREER IDEAL?
What does the company do? Why does it matter?	• Company Website's About Page • Google • LinkedIn		
What type of company is it? How many employees?	• Company Website's About Page • LinkedIn		
Who are their competitors?	• Google • LinkedIn		
Who is their leadership/ leadership team?	• Company Website's Team or Leadership Team • Google • Recent Press		

WHAT YOU WANT TO KNOW	WHERE TO START YOUR SEARCH	NOTES AND RESEARCH	HOW DOES THIS COMPARE TO YOUR SPECIFIC CAREER IDEAL?
What makes them unique?	● Company Website's About and/or Product/Services Page ● Customer Testimonials ● Social Media Channels		
Who are their clients and /or customers?	● Company Website ● Client Testimonials ● Social Media Channels		
When did the company launch?	● Company Website ● LinkedIn		
Where is the company located?	● Company Website ● LinkedIn		
Do they have other offices?	● Company Website		
What is their work culture like?	● Company Career's Page ● LinkedIn ● Glassdoor ● InHerSight ● The Muse ● Career Contessa ● Speaking with Current or Former Employees		

WHAT YOU WANT TO KNOW	WHERE TO START YOUR SEARCH	NOTES AND RESEARCH	HOW DOES THIS COMPARE TO YOUR SPECIFIC CAREER IDEAL?
What benefits do they offer?	• Company Career's Page • LinkedIn • Glassdoor • InHerSight • The Muse • Career Contessa • Speaking with Current or Former Employees		
What perks do they offer?	• Company Career's Page • LinkedIn • Glassdoor • InHerSight • The Muse • Career Contessa • Speaking with Current or Former Employees		
Recent Press	• Google • LinkedIn • Social Media Channels		

CHAPTER 17

Define What You Can't Control

Of course, not everything for working women today can be fixed with worksheets and lists—and we'd frankly be remiss, in this book and in life, to ignore the greater problems underlying our frustrations in the workplace. Women and marginalized communities face daily challenges in the office that make them feel overlooked, unheard, or, worst of all, on the outside looking in.

A recent Pew Research Center study found that 42 percent of women in the U.S. say they have faced discrimination on the job, whether it's being passed over for important assignments, earning less, or not getting proper support from those in charge. In the same survey, 54 percent of women reported unwanted, inappropriate sexual advances from male colleagues, with 30 percent of the incidents occurring in the office itself.

Even in the age of #TimesUp and #MeToo, there's still plenty of progress to be made for women in the workplace because of what we continue to be unfairly forced to confront every day: the "good old boys'" club, a pervasive "boys will be boys" mentality, a massive wage gap, companies that simply lack women in leadership positions, unconscious bias, discrimination ranging from ageism to pregnancy and motherhood to how likable we are, mansplaining in meetings, and maybe the newest member of this irritating list, gaslighting, among many others. So much to deal with, in fact, that just "dealing with it" feels like an insurmountable task. Not to mention that so much of corporate policy and programs are outside of our control.

When all feels lost at work or when you're feeling especially disillusioned, it may be helpful to turn to things you *can* control. For example, while you might not be expected to change the overall "boys' club" culture in the eighty-year-old institution where you work, you can shake things up in other ways. You can challenge a derogatory remark by asking, "Is that an appropriate thing to say?" You can celebrate the accomplishments of your underappreciated and overlooked coworkers. Both actions highlight an alternative to business as usual. Here are some other things you can do to disrupt the norm.

1. **Talk about uncomfortable/difficult topics:** Everyone has unconscious bias—even the best-intentioned people—and those interactions affect the workplace. Women (and women of color especially) face daunting roadblocks when dealing with this bias at work. Don't shy away from talking about these challenging topics. Be open to feedback and confront inequalities by talking to your colleagues, your boss, and HR, and leading by example.
2. **Celebrate employee differences:** One of the most important ways to show employees or coworkers that you respect their backgrounds and traditions is to invite them to share those in the workplace. And when they do, actively participate and engage.
3. **Be a role model—and sponsor women:** Research from Catalyst showed that almost two-thirds of women reported a lack of

senior or visibly successful female role models as a major obstacle to their career advancement. Seek out or create opportunities to have the female leaders at your company showcased. And if you're in a position to appoint highly qualified women to senior roles, do it! Sponsor women by advocating for their success and championing their progress!

4. **Learn how you can impact your workplace from the ground up:** Help organize talks, screenings, guest speakers, and open forums where you and your coworkers (including men!) can be exposed to diverse viewpoints and perspectives of more people from marginalized communities. Consider forming an inclusion council with senior leaders at your company.

5. **Support your fellow women in the workplace:** The next time a woman is getting mansplained to, interrupted, or subjected to anything that can hold her back, don't stand by. Speak up, amplify her voice, and send the ladder back down to support other women on their way up. Alternatively, when a woman at work goes above and beyond, compliment her but then go and share that with her boss. It can go a long way in gaining her the recognition she deserves.

6. **Make a social media audit and evaluate what you read:** Follow people, institutions, and publications that will ensure you're reading, seeing, and supporting diverse voices and points of view. Educate yourself on topics that are important and meaningful to otherwise underrepresented folks in your company. Advocate for them—whenever possible.

7. **Use your empathy as a weapon:** When you recognize something that's unsavory or downright unjust, speak up. Too often, we back down from battles that don't seem to be "ours" to fight. If you sense something amiss—maybe it's how a new mother is

being treated upon her return from maternity leave—step up and offer your support.

Use Your Words: The Gender Dictionary for Modern Times

Something you most certainly have control over is your own knowledge of what behavior is not acceptable out there. Here's a dictionary of terms and behaviors women need to understand and watch out for.

To summarize this tool, remember that just because you can't control something doesn't mean you can't influence change. Taking action—even if it seems small—adds up. Managing what you can control can have impact over time and provides the awareness and mind-set you can use to make successful Power Moves in the future.

PROBLEMATIC WORDS/BEHAVIOR	DEFINITION	HOW TO COMBAT IT
BENEVOLENT SEXISM	LESS OBVIOUS. KIND OF SEEMS LIKE A COMPLIMENT, EVEN THOUGH IT'S ROOTED IN MEN'S FEELINGS OF SUPERIORITY.	DON'T LET THESE COMMENTS SLIDE. WHILE THEY MIGHT NOT COME FROM AN OVERTLY "BAD" PLACE, THEY ARE DAMAGING. COMMUNICATE THAT. TAKE A PAGE FROM THE OLD MANSPLAINER AND RETORT WITH A, "WELL, ACTUALLY..."
BROPROPRIATING	STEALING AN IDEA FROM A WOMAN AND THEN MAKING IT SEEM LIKE IT WAS/IS YOUR IDEA.	ADDRESS THIS HEAD-ON. THERE IS NO EXCUSE FOR SOMEONE TAKING CREDIT FOR YOUR WORK. IF THIS HAPPENS IN A MEETING SETTING, YOU MIGHT SAY SOMETHING LIKE, "I PRESENTED THIS IDEA TO THE TEAM LAST WEEK, AND I ALSO HAD XYZ TO ADD TO IT."
CONCRETE CEILING	UNLIKE A GLASS CEILING WHERE YOU CAN SEE IT, THE CONCRETE CEILING IS A TERM TO DESCRIBE WHAT WOMEN OF COLOR FACE WHEN THEY'RE TRYING TO MOVE UP AT WORK. THEY CAN'T EVEN SEE WHAT BARRIERS ARE ABOVE THEM BECAUSE YOU CAN'T SEE THROUGH IT.	RISK-AVERSE LAYERS OF MEN NEED TO APPOINT HIGHLY-QUALIFIED WOMEN OF COLOR TO TOP POSITIONS—NOT JUST WHEN THE COMPANY IS IN TIME OF CRISIS. WOMEN OF COLOR NEED SPONSORS. THEY CAN ALSO BUILD UP THEIR OWN GROUPS WHO FACE SIMILAR CHALLENGES AND DISCUSS STRATEGIES FOR OVERCOMING THIS.
COWBOY UP. SHE TOOK IT LIKE A MAN. GROW A PAIR.	USING MALE GENITALIA TO DESCRIBE POWERFUL MOVES VERSUS FEMALE GENITALIA TO DESCRIBE WEAK MOVES.	REMOVE THIS LANGUAGE FROM YOUR VOCABULARY AND URGE OTHERS TO DO SO.
DISCRIMINATION	TREATING A GROUP OF PEOPLE UNJUST BECAUSE THEY ARE DIFFERENT CATEGORIES OF PEOPLE, ESPECIALLY ON THE GROUNDS OF RACE, AGE, OR SEX.	DON'T IGNORE IT. CALL IT OUT AND CORRECT PEOPLE WHEN THEY ARE DISCRIMINATING AGAINST YOU OR SOMEONE ELSE.

PROBLEMATIC WORDS/BEHAVIOR	DEFINITION	HOW TO COMBAT IT
EXOTICIZATION	THE PROCESS OF SEXUALIZING A GROUP, SUCH AS WOMEN, AND REDUCING THEM TO "OTHER."	DON'T REFER TO PEOPLE AS "IT" OR "OTHER."
GASLIGHTING	MANIPULATE (SOMEONE) BY PSYCHOLOGICAL MEANS INTO QUESTIONING THEIR OWN SANITY.	GASLIGHTING CAN BE A REALLY INSIDIOUS MANEUVER IN THE WORKPLACE. IF YOU FEEL THAT SOMEONE IS GASLIGHTING YOU, IT'S MORE IMPORTANT THAT YOU STAND YOUR GROUND, STATE FACTS, AND RESIST MANIPULATION.
GENDER ROLES	"GENDER ROLES ARE SETS OF CULTURALLY DEFINED BEHAVIORS SUCH AS MASCULINITY AND FEMININITY," ACCORDING TO ENCYCLOPEDIA. "IN MOST CULTURES THIS BINARY DIVISION OF GENDER IS ROUGHLY ASSOCIATED WITH BIOLOGICAL SEX – MALE OR FEMALE."	CORRECT OTHERS WHEN THEY USE GENDER-NORMATIVE LANGUAGE. NO LONGER LABEL THINGS AS EITHER MASCULINE OR FEMININE, HIM OR HER, ETC. REPLACE WITH THEY/THEM. BE MINDFUL WHEN YOU'RE REFERRING TO A PROFESSION, LIKE POLICEMAN, TO CHANGE IT TO POLICE PERSON. OR REFER TO A PROFESSION, LIKE A DOCTOR, AS "HIM."
GLASS CEILING	A BARRIER THAT WOMEN AND OTHER MINORITIES FACE, HOLDING THEM BACK FROM PROFESSIONAL ADVANCEMENT.	WHEN YOU EXPERIENCE SUCCESS, BRING ANOTHER WOMAN ALONG WITH YOU. KEEP AN OPEN DIALOGUE WITH THE FEMALE LEADERSHIP IN YOUR OWN COMPANY OR IN COMPANIES YOU ADMIRE.
HOLLOW GESTURES	MAKING CHANGES WITH ONLY WORDS AND NOT ACTIONS. FOR EXAMPLE, "WE'RE GOING TO FOCUS ON DIVERSITY HIRING" BUT THEN IT DOESN'T HAPPEN.	DON'T SAY IT IF YOU'RE NOT GOING TO FOLLOW THROUGH. HAVE AN ACTIONABLE PLAN IN PLACE THAT YOU SHARE AT THE SAME TIME AS THE COMMENT.
HOSTILE SEXISM	OVERTLY NEGATIVE IDEAS AND STEREOTYPES ABOUT A PARTICULAR GENDER.	HOSTILITY AND SEXISM HOLD NO PLACE IN THE OFFICE. THE COMBINATION SHOULD BE SWIFTLY REPORTED.

PROBLEMATIC WORDS/BEHAVIOR	DEFINITION	HOW TO COMBAT IT
INFANTILIZING LANGUAGE	USING CUTE LANGUAGE TO DOWNPLAY A WOMAN'S EXPERIENCE. FOR EXAMPLE, "OH THAT'S SO CUTE, BUT…"	CORRECT PEOPLE WHEN THEY USE THIS LANGUAGE AND SET BOUNDARIES. ALSO, LEAD BY EXAMPLE AND DON'T USE THIS LANGUAGE EITHER.
LOCKER-ROOM TALK	OFFENSIVE COMMENTS MADE BY MEN THAT ARE EXPLAINED AWAY AS SOMETHING MEN WOULD SAY IN PRIVATE TO EACH OTHER.	THIS HAS NO PLACE IN THE OFFICE. CALL OUT THE BEHAVIOR ON THE SPOT AND REPORT TO HR.
MALE GAZE	THE ACT OF DEPICTING WOMEN IN MASS MEDIA AS SEXUAL OBJECTS FOR THE PLEASURE OF MALE VIEWERS.	THIS TYPE OF BEHAVIOR HAS NO PLACE IN THE OFFICE. IF YOU SENSE THAT IT IS HAPPENING TO YOU, A COLLEAGUE, OR A CLIENT, REPORT IT.
MANSPLAINING	WHEN A MAN EXPLAINS SOMETHING TO A WOMAN IN A CONDESCENDING, OVERCONFIDENT, AND OFTEN INACCURATE OR OVERSIMPLIFIED MANNER.	WHEN SOMEONE BEGINS TO MANSPLAIN SOMETHING TO YOU, IT'S BEST TO ADDRESS IT OUTRIGHT. WHILE YOU CAN CHOOSE YOUR OWN TONE WITH WHICH TO RESPOND, IT'S BEST TO BE DIRECT IN RESPONDING BY SAYING SOMETHING LIKE, "WELL, YES, JOHN, I HAVE MY PHD IN LINGUISTICS, BUT THANKS FOR MANSPLAINING THIS TOPIC TO ME."
MANTERRUPTION	A BEHAVIOR WHEN MEN INTERRUPT WOMEN UNNECESSARILY. THIS CAN LEAD TO MEN CONTRIBUTING MORE TO A CONVERSATION THAN WOMEN.	THIS BEHAVIOR, OFTEN SEEN IN MEETING SETTINGS, CAN BE SHUT DOWN WITH A SIMPLE STATEMENT LIKE, "THANKS FOR YOUR INPUT, GENE, BUT I HAVEN'T FINISHED MY THOUGHT."
MICROAGGRESSIONS	THE SUBTLE YET HARMFUL FORMS OF DISCRIMINATORY BEHAVIOR EXPERIENCED BY MEMBERS OF OPPRESSED GROUPS.	FIND SOCIAL SUPPORT TO TALK THROUGH THESE FEELINGS. BEING VALIDATED IN HOW YOU'RE FEELING CAN HELP YOU CORRECT YOUR MICROAGGRESSOR IN THE FUTURE.

PROBLEMATIC WORDS/BEHAVIOR	DEFINITION	HOW TO COMBAT IT
MISOGYNOIR	MISOGYNY DIRECTED TOWARD BLACK WOMEN.	WHETHER YOU EXPERIENCE THIS OR WITNESS IT, IT'S CRUCIAL TO TAKE SERIOUS ACTION. DOCUMENT THE BEHAVIOR AND IMMEDIATELY BRING IT TO HUMAN RESOURCES. IF THERE ISN'T AN HR DEPARTMENT, REPORT THIS TO THE EEOC (EQUAL EMPLOYMENT OPPORTUNITY COMMISSION).
MISOGYNY	HATRED OF WOMEN.	MISOGYNY HAS A LONG HISTORY IN THE WORKPLACE, BUT THAT HISTORY IS DRAWING TO AN END. ANYTHING YOU PERCEIVE AS MISOGYNISTIC IN NATURE SHOULD BE DOCUMENTED AND REPORTED.
PERIOD/PMS-ING. SMILE MORE. RESTING BITCH FACE. CALM DOWN. OVERLY AMBITIOUS. AGGRESSIVE. BITCHY.	ALL THE THINGS INSECURE PEOPLE SAY TO WOMEN OR ABOUT WOMEN WHEN WE'RE NOT LIVING UP TO THEIR/SOCIETY'S UNREALISTIC EXPECTATIONS.	ENCOURAGE SOMEONE TO REMOVE THIS LANGUAGE FROM THEIR VOCABULARY. WHILE THESE SORTS OF PHRASES MIGHT HAVE BEEN "FUNNY" IN 1997, THEY HAVE NO PLACE IN A WORKING ENVIRONMENT.
UNCONSCIOUS BIAS	SOCIAL STEREOTYPES PEOPLE HAVE ABOUT INDIVIDUALS THAT FORM OUTSIDE THEIR OWN CONSCIOUS AWARENESS.	BECOME BETTER AT RECOGNIZING IT AND CORRECTING YOUR PATH. WHEN YOU RECOGNIZE YOUR OWN UNCONSCIOUS BIAS, ASK YOURSELF QUESTIONS AROUND WHY IT EXISTS— AND DO WORK TO SQUASH IT.
WORKING MOM. MOMMY HOURS.	REVEALS THE ASSUMPTION, OR PRESCRIPTION, THAT IT IS WOMEN WHO TAKE CARE OF KIDS.	SHUT IT DOWN. IT'S NOBODY'S BUSINESS WHO DOES WHAT IN YOUR HOUSEHOLD OR IN YOUR FAMILY. A SIMPLE, "I'D ADVISE YOU NOT TO MAKE ASSUMPTIONS ABOUT ANYBODY'S HOME LIFE" SHOULD SHUT DOWN THESE COMMENTS. IF YOU FEEL THERE IS MOTHERHOOD OR PREGNANCY DISCRIMINATION IN YOUR WORKPLACE, TAKE THIS MATTER TO HUMAN RESOURCES OR THE EEOC (EQUAL EMPLOYMENT OPPORTUNITY COMMISSION).

CHAPTER 18

Celebrate Your Mistakes as Successes

Another important tool that will help you build a career on your terms is embracing the F-word: *failure*. Too often, ambitious, achievement-focused people are afraid to discuss their mistakes and feel ashamed of any missteps. But mistakes can be a tool for advancement and an essential part of lifelong career engagement. This tool introduces ways you can embrace missteps, successfully learn from them, and start fresh with confidence.

There's an Oprah quote I love: "There is no such thing as failure. Failure is just life trying to move us in another direction." What you learn as you get further and further into your career is that our biggest mistakes are often gifts that give us the direction, course correction, or readjustment we need to move forward. Here are additional benefits of mistakes:

1. **Mistakes help us stay humble:** In our #BossedUp age of hardcharging confidence, humility is an underrated character trait. But being humble, open, and earnest, and showing vulnerability, can

help us strive to succeed in the purest of ways. Understanding when you've made a mistake and putting in the genuine effort to fix it and change your approach and behavior in the future rewires the brain. It helps keep us engaged and takes us away from our ego and into learning and acquiring real skill. Indeed, mistakes make us humble, and they make us want to get better. Earlier this year, I made a mistake by sending a marketing email to the Career Contessa email list that was out of character and left people feeling like we were trying to guilt-trip them for not buying a product. Of course, that was NOT our intention, but the marketing gurus advised us that gutsy email subject lines were the key to increasing email open rates. As if we needed another lesson in trusting our intuition, you can probably guess that it didn't go well, and we received quite a few angry responses. I felt terrible, ashamed, embarrassed, and definitely like I made a mistake. I decided to write and send a whole-hearted apology. The positive responses were overwhelming. People will not only accept your apology, but they will respect you more for owning your mistakes. Apologizing when you really mean it is different from using it as a qualifier before you state your opinion or request, or as fluff wording in an email. A genuine apology comes from a place of humility and owning your mistakes. The other comes from a place of insecurity. Let's train ourselves (and the world!) to appreciate humility more.

2. **Mistakes provide deep, lived-in experience:** How do we get better at what we do? Through experience. How do we get that experience? Not usually through our successes.

3. **Mistakes can make us smarter:** In a 2011 study on growth mind-set and post-error adjustments, researchers found that humans essentially have two distinct responses to mistakes: we either shut down or we pay more attention—and the response

we choose can mean all the difference in how the mistake will impact our lives moving forward. The study uncovered that those who shut down saw the mistake as a threat, wanted to avoid self-doubt and feeling bad, and so their brains shut off and moved on (the kinds of people who struggle to apologize after a mistake also likely fall into this camp). In this case, a mistake did not fit in with their self-image, and so they simply refused to let it in. Those who ignored mistakes and moved on to the next decision were less likely to use it to change their future behavior. But the subjects whose brains paid attention to mistakes looked at them as a kind of wake-up call (whereby the brain focused in on the negative outcome and treated it like a problem that needed solving). This group gave more attention to their next decision and tried to prevent a repeat of the mistake. This meant they were more likely to learn from the mistake. They improved. They became smarter. So how do we practically start down the road to rethinking failure?

Start from a Place of Confidence

Instead of impostor-syndrome thinking when you are approaching a scenario that is stressful or fear-inducing, imagine the result of bringing something positive to your life, no matter what that result may be. Make it your goal in every professional situation to be firmly planted in growth and learning over achievement and "success." Look at potential meetings, speeches, interviews, and presentations as opportunities to gather more information about who you are and what you can do.

Perhaps this should go without saying, but fully commit to the work itself, come prepared, and work to create a life where you are not sabotaging yourself by facilitating a negative outcome—e.g., being late, not arriving with what you need, not putting in the research or work beforehand that you need to succeed. Confidence is not created by thought alone. Confidence is created by taking action—and then doing those things that help you develop trust in yourself. Author Fran Hauser suggests something called "evidence-based confidence," which is when you write out a few examples of times when things *have* gone well—when you killed it in that presentation, received great feedback, closed the deal, etc.—and review that evidence whenever you need a confidence boost. When you develop self-trust, you feel more confident taking action. This whole cycle builds on itself.

Take Accountability

When we make a mistake, it's always easiest to point the finger and blame other people. Even in a case like getting fired, when it might not be entirely our fault or may not be due to something we've done wrong (firing is often caused by a toxic corporate culture, disorganized management, and poor fits), it's important to consider what we could have done better. Taking accountability does not mean obsessing over or using your mistakes to spiral into shame and self-loathing, it's simply acknowledging that there's room for improvement. Honestly and accurately assessing both your skills and your potential deficits is what will help you continue to find work that makes you feel satisfied and engaged.

Instead Of	Try
I'M A FAILURE	I'M HUMAN, IT'S OK TO MAKE MISTAKES
I'LL NEVER GET IT RIGHT	I NEED TO BE PATIENT WITH MYSELF AND KEEP TRYING
I'M NOT CUT OUT FOR THIS	I'LL NEVER KNOW UNLESS I TRY
EVERYONE HATES WHAT I DO	WHAT ARE PEOPLE ACTUALLY SAYING ABOUT MY WORK? HOW CAN I USE IT TO HELP ME IMPROVE?
MY BOSS HATES ME	I NEED TO FIND A WAY TO GET MY NEEDS MET IN THIS JOB – WITH OR WITHOUT MY BOSS'S APPROVAL
I'M ASHAMED	HOW CAN I TURN THIS MISTAKE INTO AN OPPORTUNITY FOR GROWTH AND LEARNING?
THEY'LL NEVER GIVE ME A GOOD ASSIGNMENT	I'LL NEVER KNOW UNLESS I ASK

Manage Your Fear of Failure

When you feel afraid of failing and see this fear becoming an obstacle to your success, play out worst-case scenarios in your head—what will happen if you attempt X and it doesn't work out? Our worst fears are usually about embarrassing ourselves and not meeting our (super-high) expectations—but what if we could get past the fear of embarrassment by reframing it as a potential price of learning? If we completely choked at that big interview or on that stage giving that speech, would that experience still have value? Of course it would! You will learn all of the things to do differently next time. Understanding that failure is part of the experience of living the life you want and redefining failure not as something to avoid but as necessary to the process of success will help you assuage your fear of its occurrence.

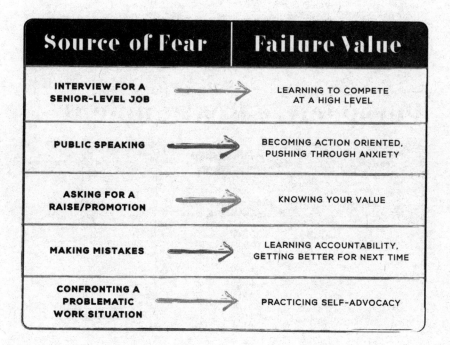

Source of Fear	Failure Value
INTERVIEW FOR A SENIOR-LEVEL JOB	LEARNING TO COMPETE AT A HIGH LEVEL
PUBLIC SPEAKING	BECOMING ACTION ORIENTED, PUSHING THROUGH ANXIETY
ASKING FOR A RAISE/PROMOTION	KNOWING YOUR VALUE
MAKING MISTAKES	LEARNING ACCOUNTABILITY, GETTING BETTER FOR NEXT TIME
CONFRONTING A PROBLEMATIC WORK SITUATION	PRACTICING SELF-ADVOCACY

Realign Your Perspective

It's common to view mistakes as negative outcomes, and yet they provide opportunities to learn and progress. Understanding this and changing your perspective can have an enormous impact on your career (and life).

Nothing happens overnight, but here's a way to realign your perspective: Write down two to three mistakes you've made in your career (or you think you've made). Then, list ways those so-called mistakes helped you affect positive change. It can be as simple as "I delivered a terrible presentation, but I learned to come more prepared to meetings." If the mistake is still fresh, write down ways you can use it in your favor, such as "I delivered a terrible presentation, so I'm going to sign up for Toastmasters to learn how to be a better speaker in public.

This will ultimately help my career long-term beyond company meetings."

Perspective Realignment

MISTAKE	POSITIVE CHANGE FOR MISTAKE	ACTION
EX: I delivered a terrible presentation.	I learned to come to meetings more prepared.	I'm going to sign up for Toastmasters to learn how to be a better speaker in public.

So, mistakes make us smarter—they teach us new, improved ways to approach projects, assignments, and even life. They help us stay humble. When you've made a mistake, don't let your ego take control. Do your best to fix the mistake in the appropriate ways. If you don't make mistakes, you don't learn.

CHAPTER 19

Her Name Is Self-Advocacy— and She's Badass

Self-advocacy, the ability to ask for what you need or want out of work, can be one of the biggest struggles for women in their careers. But work without self-advocacy often leaves us feeling, at best, underused and fatigued and, at worst, exploited and completely fried. I'm thinking of "The Tiara Syndrome" here, a term first coined by Negotiating Women founders Carol Frohlinger and Deborah Kolb, but also referenced by Sheryl Sandberg in *Lean In*. The Tiara Syndrome is essentially the idea that women imagine if they keep doing their jobs well someone will notice them and place a tiara on their heads, that there will be a reward for simply doing the work well, without their ever having to self-advocate, speak up, or ask for recognition—all of which has been disproved by research.

Learning to speak up for yourself, having the courage and learning the skills necessary to communicate your needs in constructive ways, is one of the most powerful tools you can add to your professional arsenal, something that will require investment up front and reap rewards for years to come. At its best, self-advocacy is grown-up, intentional, proactive. It allows you to showcase your work and value in thoughtful, persuasive, reasonable ways. Learning to advocate for yourself at work and take action means you will be consistently moving toward something, never allowing yourself to stagnate or become complacent. Remember that your next move is your best move—no matter what, it's something moving you forward. Here are some ways to start thinking about self-advocacy—and implementing it into your life today.

Self-Advocacy Is Good for You— and Good for Business

Self-advocacy is not usually about storming the gates or delivering a grand or dramatic hero's speech. It's knowing what you want to communicate (career growth, an issue on a project, a problem with a boss or coworker) or what you're asking for (a raise, a promotion) and planning out the most streamlined way to advocate for this. It also means putting things in perspective, taking the ten-thousand-foot view and understanding that the happier you are at work, the more engaged you will be; that engaged, happy employees are more productive; and that increased productivity is better for businesses overall.

Also, by learning to self-advocate, to be proactive about your standing and progress in the company or project you're working on, you take pressure off your employers. By asking for what you want, clearly and maturely, you take out the guesswork and make their jobs as managers easier, freeing them up to do other, high-level work. Smart self-advocacy is a win for you, but it's almost always a win for the business you contribute to as well.

Self-Advocacy Means Sharing Your Work

This is the place where, yes, I'm telling you to: SHOUT. YOUR. ACCOMPLISHMENTS. Don't be shy or meek about your skills or what you genuinely, fully know how to do. Your boss or client should know what you're working on, the progress of this work, the ways in which you're meeting your goals or meeting a project deadline, how this relates to the company's goals, the successes you've had, the extra work you've put in, the coups you've pulled off. *Bragging about your triumphs or skills is not a bad thing.* Confidence is contagious, and when you convey confidence, the people you're working for will feel more confident too.

Self-advocacy also works in the opposite way, which means making sure to alert the people who need to know when there's a problem, when an assignment is going off course, when you need help. Suffering in silence is not the way to go—keeping silent, waiting until the last (often too late to fix anything) minute to sound an alarm, will not earn you any credit, but it will make the people in charge less likely to trust your judgment in the future.

Self-Advocacy Is Strategic

Here's a common story you've either seen or lived through. Person A gathers up the courage to address a specific request, issue, or concern—all hail the very inspiring TED Talk Person A listened to that morning! Person A sets up a time to discuss with their boss, announces their request, and then . . . that's where the plan to self-advocate ends. Person A immediately regrets their decision, and advocating in the future is shadowed by that experience.

Being an effective champion for yourself, your work, and your career is not just about identifying the problem, it's about being strategic and knowing the best solutions based on your individual needs and the needs of your company. It's about understanding what you want ideally and what you'll accept realistically. It's being able to sustain your resolve through outlining not only the situation at hand, but what you believe should be done about it. A good boss or client will appreciate and reward this effort—you've helped them by doing some of the legwork!—while a bad one may never have been able to help you solve your problem in the first place.

So, first things first: Make a plan. Write down what you're requesting or the message you'd like to have heard and practice it aloud a few times. Plan a time when the recipient can be calm and focused. When you start the conversation, stick to the facts as much as possible. Keep the conversation upbeat if you can. Don't complain, blame, or criticize. Don't get distracted. Know your desired outcome and steer the conversation toward it. Don't meander; don't self-deprecate. Learn to feel comfortable asking for what you want or explaining what you need in clear, direct, concise terms. If you're looking to take gradual steps toward a meeting with your boss, you can start by getting your boss in the habit of saying yes to you on smaller projects today, such as "Can I sit in on your meeting?" or "I'd love to include XYZ talking points in today's meeting."

Let's meet a real example of self-advocacy with Michelle Hickox. Hickox was a public accountant who asked for (and got!) summers off for ten years so she could raise her kids before leaving to become a bank CFO. I love her story because it represents self-advocacy at its best: Hickox identified what she needed and asked for it, and her career wasn't penalized in the process. When I heard about her story, I needed to know *how* she did it—here's how.

Hickox's accounting firm was small, local, and filled with either male colleagues who had stay-at-home wives or women who didn't have children. When Hickox got married and found out she was expecting, her husband decided to find a job that was more family-friendly, which included flexibility so he could pick up their daughters from day care; however, when Hickox's eldest daughter was finishing kindergarten, Hickox was left with a dilemma on what to do with child care over the summer.

Hickox knew she was a great employee, so she went to the two partners and worked out a deal that was supposed to be just for that summer, where she said, "Hey, I have this issue with child care. I would like to take from Memorial Day through the middle of August off and stay at home with my kids." Public accounting, at that point in time anyway, really was more seasonal, so she didn't have a lot of clients or client work during the summer. It was mostly administrative and training. In exchange, Hickox offered to give up her bonus. She pointed out that at the time, her bonus wasn't that big of a deal, but, in the end, they didn't take her up on that. They just let her do it. During that time frame, though, the partners also sold their local firm to a national firm, so when Hickox wanted to make this a regular thing, she had to negotiate with new leadership.

First, she checked to see if her new firm had any policies in place around flexible work schedules. While they did have policies in place, nobody really used them, and they were not supported, which is similar to a lot of policies in workplaces today. Another challenge was that Hickox's new managing partner was not supportive of any kind of flexibility—and definitely not supportive about her request. She then went to one of her original partners to discuss her request and "was basically prepared to resign and leave because I had already started talking to another firm that was willing to let me work the schedule I wanted." The original partner replied with, "You know, Michelle, this has been an issue. We already had a couple of ladies who work part-time for us. The biggest part of this negotiation is discussing how we're going to handle the other two ladies, but we really want you to stay. For us, having you 80 percent of the time is better than having you zero percent of the time." Hickox realized her leverage—she was a benefit to the company with her experience and skills.

The original partner ended up supporting Hickox's ask with the new managing partner. Even though he wasn't on board (he spent two hours over lunch telling Hickox what a bad idea it was), he agreed to do it because of the buy-in of the other partner and because Hickox had a client that the firm needed her to work on.

Hickox's request also required a "give" on her side. By going to an 80 percent schedule, she also went to an 80 percent salary. Hickox says that what almost killed this whole deal was the secrecy from the other employees. At first, the managing partner asked her to keep it a secret because he was worried everyone would ask for the same thing, but Hickox says that by keeping it a secret, it actually made people think she was just leaving early and slacking off.

Hickox went back to the managing partner and said, "Hey, this is not going to work if I can't communicate this to all of my coworkers and clients." This transparency worked well for everyone, and she continued to grow her career at that accounting firm until she eventually left for a major Power Move—becoming the CFO of a public bank that she's helped grow to become the fourth-largest bank in Texas.

Hickox acknowledges that she was able to continue her career growth because her accounting firm did eventually value their employees having families and they didn't want them to have to choose between the two, but I would argue that's partly due to

Hickox paving the road as an example. So, to make partner at her accounting firm, she got clear on the three things she needed to be good at and made sure that when she did pull back her hours, she still focused on those three things.

Hickox's story provides actionable tips (and inspiration!) that we can all follow, whether you're advocating for a flexible schedule or something else. Next time you're getting ready to self-advocate, remember these tips:

- Be a good employee to start with.
- You probably have more leverage than you think (i.e., most people want you to stay—in the job or on the project).
- Identify what you have to barter: bonus, clients, being there for the busy season, etc.
- Create a detailed plan and consider company policies.
- Find a senior sponsor to support your plan.
- Don't keep it a secret from your team or clients.
- Get clear on your three priorities needed to continue to grow in your role.

Most important, self-advocacy sets you up to make Power Moves that allow you to build a career on your terms.

CHAPTER 20

Become Your Own Career Coach

Career direction and growth at work are not only nice to have, they're imperative. They keep you engaged, excited, relevant, and on the right path. They're the secret sauce that allows you to move more fluidly through work transitions; to create and seize new opportunities; to anticipate your own needs; to challenge yourself; and to stay vibrant, plugged in, and alive at work, instead of empty inside.

Back in 2013, one of the biggest reasons I felt compelled to launch Career Contessa (and, honestly, change the entire course of my life in the best possible way) was because I was seeing a huge gap in career development resources for women—a lack of training and growth opportunities for them as employees, a lack of support as they transitioned into more senior roles and needed to acquire more senior skills, and a definite dearth of learning tools and guidance when/if they wanted to shift focus, or maybe delve into a different direction altogether—and I wanted to fill this gap in smart, thoughtful, accessible ways.

Specifically, I wanted to help women find more/better/smarter career management solutions so they could start to take action in their professional lives and identify, meet, and even exceed goals they hadn't even imagined possible. Active career management can also allow you to opt in and out of work on your terms more easily. Remember: you don't have to constantly lean in—if you want to lean out for a while, these Power Moves are how you will continue to grow your career on your terms.

Most people will switch jobs, on average, twelve times during the course of their lifetimes. Which means they'll need help pivoting, rebooting, or rebuilding from wherever they are and with whatever they've got. Career management is really just building a professional map, a path that will help you glide to the next phase and the next after that. Effective management is also individualized and timely and never one-size-fits-all. It's keeping in mind the needs of a specific person—in this case, *you*—at a specific time. It's a skill and outlook that you can teach yourself—once you know where to look.

While it's true that in the years since Career Contessa was launched, certain things have gotten *somewhat* better at *some* companies, most career management still feels like a DIY enterprise. Few organizations offer it, and those that do rarely offer it in a way that works optimally for their employees. Historically, companies tended to invest in training and broadening the skills of their workforce, particularly those in senior management. Big corporations not only offered, but recommended and highly valued supplemental training for managers; they sent employees to conferences, offered them in-office education, and were more apt to encourage apprenticeship. But today, in workplaces across the country, little is offered in the way of career management, and what is offered, you often need to find or sort out on your own, with little support (for example, how would you know that your company has a tuition reimbursement plan if you weren't told and didn't know to ask?).

In an ideal world, your company would want to foster your career growth: they'd carve out time and offer incentives for managers to mentor, give immediate feedback, and prioritize the developmental needs and training of their teams. But, since you can't expect anyone to take on this monumentally important task for you, here's what you need to know to be your own effective career coach.

Remember It's the Company, Not the Job

This is one of the most important truths I can share—whether or not you are satisfied by the work you do, whether or not you find joy in the actual tasks you complete and the skills you flex every weekday, depends greatly on who you are working with and for. Sure, there are *some* situations where you genuinely hate the duties at hand, when your core competencies are not being put to their best use, but for the most part, the reason you hate your work is because your boss is terrible, the company culture is soul-sucking and toxic, or you are undervalued, overworked, and/or treated with disrespect or disdain. Trust me, you could be doing the exact same job you are today at a different company or for a different client and instead of dreading work you'd find that you missed it when you're gone. So many employees put so much emphasis on trying to solve the problem of *what* they do without ever wondering if the issue is *where* they're doing it. Here's an exercise to start fixing that now.

Company Versus Job Exercise

How do you know if you should make a Power Move—quit your job and find something else in the same field or consider an entirely new career? Ask yourself the following questions:

1. Do you feel your work is valued?
2. Are you able to grow in your current job?
3. If you could advance in your current company, would you?
4. Do you admire the people you report to?
5. Are you still learning at your job?
6. Do you believe in the company's mission?
7. Are your concerns about projects or issues heard? Are they resolved?

If you answered "no" to more than three of the above questions—and you value the work you do—the problem is most likely with the company, not the job. It's time to start thinking about a Power Move.

Play to Your Strengths

This is what's most likely *not* going to happen: you're not going to walk into your boss's office one day, ask a broad question about where you are professionally and where you should be or what you should do next, and have your boss give you the magic solution for a long and purposeful career. Unfortunately, your boss is not a Magic 8-Ball—you can't shake the answers for your future out of her. That's because the job of managers is to focus on the overall performance of their team, which involves more than just you. They have little to no ability to be fortune-tellers and sometimes are not even good advice givers when it comes to individual careers, for obvious reasons: their interest in you is focused on their needs. But that's okay; you don't need a Magic 8-Ball—you are in charge of your own career future.

From countless interactions, I've learned that leveraging strengths is a key to future career moves. Strengths are important because people who use their strengths every day are six times more likely to be engaged on the job, and we all want that. Surprisingly, according to Gallup, research also shows that people who use their strengths are 8 percent more productive and 15 percent less likely to quit their jobs. The obvious conclusion: planning a future based on your strengths is the smart thing to do. You'll experience more engagement, opportunity, and career fulfillment. Your strengths are essentially your competitive advantage.

So, Ms. Career Coach, how do you even begin identifying your strengths? First, understand what strengths are not. Strengths are not your interests or passions. They are skills (and applicable knowledge) that make you uniquely valuable in the workplace and differentiate you from your peers. One way to identify your strengths is to answer these two questions.

1. What are you good at that's required for your job? Where have you had success at work so far? What have others told you you're good at?
2. What gives you energy at work or when do you feel the most energized? Where do you enjoying spending your time?

Compare your answers to both questions, and where they overlap is a good indication of a unique strength. Once you know what your strengths are, create more opportunities where you can use them. Those opportunities provide the "evidence" you'll want/need to help guide future career moves. For example, if a strength of yours is building relationships, what are some other creative ways that you can use that strength? Identify those opportunities, go after them, and now you'll have more "evidence" of this strength in action. That evidence allows you to approach your boss with concrete examples to back up why they should promote you to build a relationship with that essential client or, even better, provides you with clarity on why you're ready to accept that new job in business development. While I love tests that tell you your strength's domains or themes, that doesn't mean a whole lot in the real world if you don't know how to apply them or talk about them as they relate to work. That's why I prefer this two-question approach to determining your strengths. Communicating what your strengths are in a way that can be applied in the workplace is also critical to leveraging those strengths at work—and ultimately becoming a person who creates goals with their strengths in mind.

Set and Manage Career Goals

Even if your boss has their own goals for you (but especially if they don't), begin a running list of everything you'd like to achieve at work in the next quarter, the next six months, and the next year. This could be milestones like a raise or a promotion, but could also be smaller, quieter things like learning a new internal system or taking lead on your own project or attending more high-level meetings.

The key to managing your career with goals is to monitor progress and honestly, regularly, appraise your performance. A Career Contessa reader, Cameo Pierce, recently shared with me that she makes every Friday "Career Development Friday" and blocks off two to three p.m. on her calendar to reflect on her career goals and then fill any gaps. This could mean reading about a specific topic that relates to her goals, gathering feedback, online learning, or really anything that helps her get out of a planning mode and move her career forward.

Dedicating time each week is valuable because it also keeps you aware of your time frame. If you don't accomplish a goal within the time frame you've established, you need to reflect on why that happened and what you could have done differently. A helpful way to set goals is to make them S.M.A.R.T. This stands for Specific, Measurable, Attainable, Realistic, and Timely. The worksheet below can help you establish and leverage your goals.

Understand When and How You'll Be Evaluated

What are the goals of your position? Which are your relevant KPIs (key performance indicators)? You'll be considered successful when _____ happens? It's critical to have clear expectations about what comprises success in any role you're in so you know where you stand and can track your performance, and, ultimately, do what's needed to achieve what you want (more responsibility, a bigger paycheck, another project with this client). In an ideal world, these goals, responsibilities, expectations, and benchmarks would be set by your manager and outlined for you in clear, consistent ways, but if they're not—ask for them to be! Get proactive and go to your boss with suggestions of what you think should be expected for your role. Be prepared with a general outline—

Create SMART Goals

Complete the following chart for each goal you want to set right now.
The more concrete detail you can add, the better.

	GOAL #1	GOAL #2	GOAL #3
SPECIFIC Why do you want to achieve this goal?			
MEASURE How will you know you accomplished your goal?			
ATTAIN What will be the action items you need to take?			
REALISTIC Is this realistic within your timeframe?			
TIMELY When do you want to accomplish this by?			

· Bonus ·

BARRIERS List all the obstacles in your way.			
RESOURCES What tools are necessary?			

including stretch goals—and work with your boss to come up with a concrete plan. If your boss isn't 100 percent sure of your KPIs, then try to determine your own by asking lots of questions. The more questions you ask, the more your boss will share what matters most to her. Then, when you're prioritizing your work, make sure to consider that information.

Track Your Progress

Whether they're bullet or vision, high-tech digital or painstakingly handwritten, there are few things I love more than a journal. This is especially true for a daily work journal, which can give you the opportunity to reflect and celebrate your progress and small wins at work.

In the book *The Progress Principle*, authors Steven Kramer and Teresa Amabile show how small wins can help create forward momentum. This momentum is what helps ignite your own engagement with your work and career. Keeping a daily journal on office life and your own personal career progress is imperative to keeping track of your growth, your wins and losses, to understanding yourself and how your skills and point of view shift, contort, and expand over time. Work journaling can not only help you become more efficient and goal-oriented, but it can also help you gain perspective on the interpersonal challenges at work too. You'll get the opportunity to examine the times you felt most vulnerable and those when you felt most powerful, along with the circumstances that surrounded each of the two.

For those of us who are data nerds (raises hand!), work journals provide a long view of our habits and behaviors; they can help us identify patterns and bring more clarity to issues for which, in the moment, we feel most frustrated or confused by. Want to keep a work journal but don't know where to begin? Here are a few basic questions that Career Contessa contributor Elana Lyn Gross recommends to help you get started:

1. What is one lesson (or lessons, if you have many!) that I learned today?
2. Did anyone compliment or comment on my work today? What did they say? (Bonus: This makes it easier to remember your accomplishments when you want to ask for a raise or promotion!)
3. What is one big thing that I accomplished today?
4. Did I do anything above and beyond my basic job description today?
5. What is one way that I can go above and beyond tomorrow?

I know you're busy, but even if you can only fit this in once a week, this exercise will help you reflect, focus, and consider the big picture of your career, and that will be well worth it.

Commit to Improve

A commitment to career improvement is one of the best ways to open the door of opportunity because it can help enhance existing strengths and/or develop new ones. However, it never happens on its own. Even though it takes effort and time that you probably don't think you have, there are more career improvement options than ever to fit your budget, learning style, and career stage.

Some examples at your company might include formal mentoring, job shadowing, employee growth or skill-building programs, or even tuition reimbursement. Outside your company you have access to podcasts, books, conferences, online communities, and online learning courses. If a physical space is more your thing, consider joining a coworking space or organization you can get involved in that offers career development programming. Contact local business and networking groups—or even local colleges—where you may be able to audit or attend sessions for cheap or even free.

Stop the Comparison Game

If you're struggling to appreciate where you are right now, maybe you're too deep into the comparison game, fixated on and obsessing about how "stuck" you feel, while others around you are thriving. You may think about this issue all day and into the night with no real solution. You may believe you will "always" feel like this and "never" get out.

I am here to tell you that you can break with the myth of comparison. Stop focusing on what others have by focusing on what you yourself have and creating habits that help you break this pattern of comparison. The steps to reset your own career perception aren't always easy, but a change in perspective is absolutely necessary to move forward. Start by writing down all the negative feelings you have about your work and all the negative ways you're comparing yourself to others. Things like: "I'm not as far as I wanted to be in my career by twenty-eight" or "I'll never make as much money as I wanted."

Then, revise those statements with more positive approaches/an action plan. For instance, "I am twenty-eight and have plenty of time to figure my career out. I am working on that, starting now" and "In order to make more money, I need a raise. I'm going to start planning to ask for one."

Additionally, here are some daily/weekly things you might find helpful:

- Recognize your triggers and label them. This is a great way to stop feelings of comparison before they start.
- Keep a gratitude jar and place a note inside of one thing you feel grateful for each day. Read them all at the end of the week.
- Set limits for all of your social media apps each day—a deep well of "compare and despair" for most of us. If you find yourself exceeding your limits, remove the apps from your phone altogether.
- Use comparison as motivation to improve. If you're envious of what someone else has, examine that, and, if it's healthy motivation, use it as a guide for what you want. For example, maybe you're envious of someone's promotion, but when you examine it, you're envious of how well she advocates for herself. How can you use her example as fuel for your future advocating?
- Volunteer your time to a community organization. Through an experience helping others, you'll often have more appreciation for your own progress, life, career, and more.

"Busyness" Can Affect Your Work

It's true, busyness can actually have an adverse effect on one's work—which makes you nearly incapable of working—and it elevates levels of stress, which makes your work suffer. A recent study by the American Psychological Association found that the majority of adults in the US experience stress levels that exceed those necessary to maintain proper health—workers in the study expressed a desire to bring down their stress levels, but there was a catch: they said they were too busy to address them.

Busyness can be a real, actual addiction like dependency on drugs or alcohol, and becoming motivated by it can warp how you work and cause you to form poor habits—adding mundane busywork to your schedule, overcomplicating projects, hoarding tasks instead of delegating, all in order to make you feel like you're doing more, checking more boxes, crossing more things off a seemingly endless to-do list.

Having a need to be "busy" for busyness's sake can also limit your ability to grow and advance in your career. Those fresh ideas you're dying to present to your boss? Well, neuroscientists found that innovation and insight only come in a relaxed, diffused mode. Our brain works in two modes: diffused/daydreaming and concentrated/focused thought. The fresh ideas come during the diffused mode, which also explains why your best ideas might come while you're in the shower.

When you're constantly "on" and in that hyperfocused busy mode, you can fall into "tunneling," which means your cognitive capacity for what you can think about narrows. You're putting yourself in a place where you can really only focus on the low-value tasks right in front of you. This can lead you to crowd your schedule with basic but time-consuming tasks, instead of searching for more meaningful, high-quality work or better, more innovative ways to complete your existing work. Crowding your life with busyness can make you inefficient, a major career impediment if you desire to get ahead. Perhaps most important, embracing constant busyness can keep you from engaging in and facing the issues and challenges in your own life, from deep introspection to cultivating and maintaining personal relationships to developing quality self-care routines and doing things you love and enjoy outside of work.

How can you break your busyness habits? Here are some examples:

1. **Stop talking about being busy:** Start by removing "I'm so busy" from your vocabulary and when someone asks, "How are you?" try talking about what you're actually doing—the specific things, projects, accomplishments that you're currently working on.

2. **Analyze your schedule over the course of a week:** Notice when you are getting real work done versus the optics of "busyness"— are there weekly meetings or calls that you don't need to attend? Tasks you've added that may be filler for your day? What do you absolutely need to continue doing and what work can you let go?

3. **Embrace leisure time:** We're so great at multitasking that we now have trouble embracing leisure, and worst of all, we feel guilty (remember FOND from earlier?) when we do embrace leisure. I'm here to give you 100 percent permission to binge-watch Bravo without feeling like you need to also be checking email, meal prepping, etc. Fully engaging in a leisure activity allows you to have a distinct "off" period in your day/week.

4. **Audit your office hours:** Are you staying late or arriving early just for face time? Or do you absolutely have to stay until seven p.m.? Leaving the office on time each day can greatly improve your well-being by freeing up time for exercise, home-cooked meals, and drinks out with friends.

5. **Delegate tasks:** Some people really are struggling to get everything done in a day, and when they're told to delegate, it feels like adding one more thing to their to-do list. To simplify this process, write down one to three things you did that day that you could have delegated. This could be work tasks but also home/family/personal tasks too. It's much less intimidating to reflect on everything you did in the last twenty-four hours versus the running list of things you do each week or month. According to *Learning Solutions*, research has shown that we forget

70 percent of new information within twenty-four hours and 90 percent of information within one week.

6. **If you're the boss, lead by example:** Set the standard for your employees—work efficiently during the day and leave on time as often as you can.

7. **Scrutinize your busyness:** Are you using how busy you are in and of itself as a measure of success? How much is your busyness a posture? How much of it is real?

8. **Prioritize efficiency:** Are your work tools all up-to-date? Are there simple technologies, habits, or shortcuts you could use to get your work done faster? Start with something small, like optimizing the way you use email, and build up to apps or services that can save you time. One of my favorites is using a calendar tool like Calendly to schedule calls.

9. **Take time to slow down:** Check in with your body several times throughout the day. Are your shoulders tense? Are you able to breathe slowly? Check in with your attitude and realize that relaxing is a feat too, but it can be a more rewarding action than busyness.

10. **Book a weekly appointment with yourself:** Block out time during the workday each week that's just for you—even if it's just insisting on a real lunch break or time to take a walk outside. When and if you can, use breaks during the day to read a book, journal, sit in a coffee shop and people watch—something that has nothing at all to do with work. Remember that doing anything well requires you to focus on your wellness first.

Despite a cultural glamorization of "busyness," it's not an indication of productivity or even achievement. Rejecting busyness for busyness's sake, and prioritizing efficiency instead, will actually make you more productive at work.

Big-Picture Thinking Is a Red Flag

When you imagine yourself as a successful person, when you day-dream about who you'll be and what you'll wear and what speeches you'll give and whom you'll talk to, you probably feel pretty great. Though this life isn't real yet (and might never be), dreaming to the point of distraction can be a major career impediment.

Instead of getting lost imagining what you want your life to be, start tuning in to your life now. How do your current experiences relate to your long-term goal? Throw away the five-year plan and ask yourself, "What do I want to do tomorrow? What have I done that I've enjoyed and that I'd like to do more of?" Real, sustained achievement is about combining our inherent skills and the things that give us energy with a career where they'll be best suited.

So much of this career game is just discovering what gives you energy, plus what you are good at, and then following the bread crumbs to get you where you want to be. For example, a random assignment led me to a recruiting job at Hulu, which led me to realize how few companies were investing in career development, which led me to, ultimately, become founder of Career Contessa.

Remember, your value defines the path of your career. Make sure you're investing in yourself, in your core skills, in a foundation to a working life that will span decades. By taking the initiative and taking your career into your own hands, you're empowering yourself, setting yourself up for success, and honing the ability to thrive for years to come.

CHAPTER 21

Embrace Your Inner Questioner, Quester, *and* Quitter

What happens if you're actively engaging in all of the above—embracing failure, taking accountability, developing your skills, being radically introspective, examining the failings of your company and not internalizing them—but still *something is wrong*? Something is wrong with work and you don't know exactly what it is, but right before you, ever-present around you, there's a big looming question: Should you quit? And if so, what the hell are you going to do? How big of a change do you really need to make?

This is the moment when we get to use all the lessons in this book to help you decide, a moment when you need to shake off your old feelings and blocks about work and what you can and can't do (your fear of change, your stigmas surrounding taking control and going after what you want) and start opening your mind to new possibilities. Quitting is not negative! Quitting is not a failure! Quitting can be proactive and empowering and the first step in fulfilling your next best dream. Here are some common signs it's time to move on from your job or career.

The Job Doesn't Fit Your Life

The hours are long, and you need to be at home more to support a sick loved one; the job requires constant travel and you never see your kid; you have a bully at work who is keeping you from moving forward even after countless talks and behavior changes; the job is high-profile, and you hate being in the spotlight (or the opposite: the job keeps you hidden deep internally, and you want to be front-facing); the position was supposed to be one thing, turned out to be another, and you are not playing to (or in some cases even *using*) your strengths, or . . . the list goes on. Contrary to what you may think or may have been told, all of these are perfectly good reasons to leave a job—and even an industry. That's because putting yourself (and your family, if you have one) first and making your life needs a priority is a perfectly solid reason to want to make a career change.

Women often think they have to suck up discomfort, have to be "good," and that being good means that the only way they can leave a perfectly reasonable (or even high-quality) job is if the building they work in is literally on fire. They feel they must justify a decision, instead of asserting that the job is just not serving their needs. But this is one of the primary ways women get stuck in their careers, get burned out, lose zeal for work. By sucking it up and enduring sustained unhappiness, they forget what they liked about work in the first place. It's okay to question whether a "good" job is actually good for you—and if it's not, it's okay (and preferable even!) to take steps to get yourself in a better place.

The Job Is Messing with Your Health

Is a toxic work culture, a demanding schedule, a hideous commute, an angry boss, or a mismanaged company leaving you anxious, drained of energy, unable to sleep, or constantly fighting off colds? Chronic stress has been shown to impact our health in dangerous ways—from temporary illness to chronic health problems. Your health is a priority. If you aren't feeling well, chances are you aren't functioning at full capacity. Take a good hard look at your situation. Risking the health of your body and mind just isn't worth it, and there *are* careers out there that won't leave you feeling like you have to risk it.

You Need More Money

Here's the math: There are forty hours in the standard workweek. If you cannot make enough to support your life in those forty hours, you are going to have to steal hours from other parts of your life to make it up—from family obligations, from enjoying friends, from exercise, from sleep, and more. Ideally, you should make all the money you need in a full-time job. If you don't, you will grow resentful—longer hours and bigger projects will feel unfair if your salary is not commensurate with the time, effort, and results you put into your role. This also goes for a lack of benefits. Calculate the money you need to make your job livable (meaning, what you *actually* need to live, not things you'd like, like a condo by the beach or a monthly Tesla payment), ask for what you need, and if it's not offered, use this as an opportunity to move on.

You're Living a Dream That Is Not Your Own

Maybe your parents always wanted you to be a lawyer, so you went to law school and you find you hate law. Maybe your partner likes the idea of you being a doctor, so you're toiling away in med school with no real passion for it. Maybe your favorite professor told you you'd be a *great* teacher, but when you got into the job, you discovered it was not actually for you. These situations are a double whammy of stuckness—not only are you unhappy, but you may feel obliged to stick with it so you don't let someone else down. The guilt of not meeting the expectations of someone you love and/or respect compounds the dissatisfaction, which, combined with a fear that you've wasted all this time and money and training, makes you feel like you "have to" stay. But few good decisions are based in "have tos" or "shoulds"! This is not wasted time; this is learning time. You now know what you don't want, which is a first step to discovering what you do.

There's No Room for Advancement

You've done your best self-advocating for a promotion, you've spoken to your boss or HR about your willingness to take on new challenges and asked what's possible in terms of growth. But you've received no positive direction and perhaps no answers at all. Months go by like this; you nudge, but no one is willing or able to give you something new to get you excited about work again, to reward you for the hard work you've put in and the initiative you've taken. You feel undervalued, taken for granted, lost in the shuffle. You're growing bored and more complacent by the day.

There Is Room for Advancement, but You Don't Want It

Even if you could advance at this company, you don't want to. You see the people in senior management, and they are not what you aspire to. You don't want to be a top cheese at this company, and frankly you don't want to be a cheese at all. The vision of a promotion and working at this company, or in this field, for years to come feels like nothing more than a slow march to the grave.

If any of these scenarios exist, it's probably time to move on, it's imperative that you move on, you must move on or you'll keep yourself stuck longer than you want to be, longer than you ever imagined being. If you're completely burned out and feeling lost, consider taking time off to regroup (research if your company has paid sabbaticals)—even taking an intentional, reflective, unplugged vacation or staycation could help. Your goal is to gain clarity on what you're really craving so you can set yourself up to take just one courageous, actionable step toward change and achieving a new goal. Understand what you're craving with a career audit. It can help you make a more informed decision about where it will be best to land next. Here's how to do that.

1. **Honestly assess everything:** Now's the time to reflect on your interests, your past successes, times you've felt most engaged and

loved work the most. Honestly assess everything you've ever done, projects you've crushed, skills you've flexed the best—examine it all, no matter how big or small: Did you like playing point with that client on that thing? Did you feel connected and truly excellent at that one volunteer teaching position you did that one time? Were you happier in a small place or a giant corporation? What is your "core competency"? What are you best at? Is it also what you like the most? What did you want to be when you grew up? Why were you excited about the job in the first place? Does your career align with your value system—how could it?

2. **Start talking—to everyone:** Making a career change can be terrifying, but you don't have to be burdened by it all alone; you can call in reinforcements. Like Claudine Cazian, whom you read about in the Power Women, Power Moves chapter, brainstorm ideas with people you trust and who know you well—friends, family, former colleagues, even clients/vendors/partners, etc., with whom you worked closely. Ask them what *they* think you excel at, what they could see you doing. Imagine that you're on a scavenger hunt and everything is a clue. Write everything down and start comparing notes. Alexandra Dickinson, founder of Ask For It and salary negotiation expert, created her own version of this and called it a "listening tour." Here's an example of what she sent to her network:

> *Subject Line: I'm on a career listening tour. Can I ask you 2 questions?*
>
> *Hi Name,*
>
> *I'm reaching out because I'm on a career listening tour of the professional connections I most admire and respect as*

I determine what roles to pursue. I'm doing some research to prepare for my next career move and [insert why you're reaching out to them].

Would you be willing to have a 20-minute conversation with me so I can get your perspective on two questions?

1. [Insert the skills you enjoy most and even an example of where/when you used them.] When you hear this, what roles or individuals does it make you think of?
2. Is there anyone else you think I should speak with about this topic?

Thank you! Please let me know your availability for the week of XX.

I've also included a quick summary of my background:

[Insert background information.]

Best,
Name

3. **If your family and friends are not helpful, consider reaching out to a professional—a good career coach can help assess your situation and offer valuable, actionable advice:** We have a career coaching service at Career Contessa with pre-vetted experts you can explore too. Once you have even a fuzzy idea of what you might like to do next, ask your network for warm introductions and/or search LinkedIn for people in these professions and set up as many informational interviews as you can. You might get a lot of nos or zero responses, but keep at it. Remember, over

50 percent of my LinkedIn requests ignored me, but the thirty informational interviews I did get helped provide clarity and insights that refined my job search targets and improved my interview skills.

4. **Take the path of least resistance—a new position in your current industry:** Are there ways to marry whatever industry knowledge you've already built with the new work you'd like to do? For example, maybe you're employed by a marketing firm and understand the ins and outs of quality marketing, but you'd much rather work in recruiting quality candidates. Maybe you're a teacher at a private school, but you'd love the chance to go into fund-raising. One of my past coworkers in recruiting was able to transition into a general marketing role at our current company by scheduling networking lunches, working with her current manager, and making it well-known to the marketing team that she wanted to join them. Within six months, she made her desired transition, and now, a few years later, she's the director of marketing for a growing start-up. Look first within your current company—are there positions you might enjoy if given the chance? What are some skills you can stretch from what you're doing now to what you'd like to do next? Before you quit, look for opportunities to acquire new skills in your current job and, potentially, a title change that reflects these skills, both of which could set you in a new direction later on.

To keep us on track—remember, this book, and specifically this section about career management tools, is here to shift your thinking about what it means to take control of your career. You're not as stuck as you might feel. You really can be your own career coach. This is a message I'll keep repeating. With newfound (or refreshed) career awareness, you're ready to make the necessary Power Moves and have the career you want.

You can stop falling victim to the most notorious career traps or focusing your energy on what's beyond your control. As your own career coach, it's time to start believing in you. A little self-advocacy will go a long way. Embrace your own voice, meet your career challenges head-on, and use your new awareness mind-set to manage a career that can adapt and flourish in a future still to be defined.

CHAPTER 22

The Big Look

Whether you quit your job, are returning to the workforce after time away, or "other" circumstances prevailed, it's likely that at some point in your career you'll be looking for work. And, deep breath, it's not unexpected. In fact, it's perfectly normal. Consider this again—research from the Bureau of Labor Statistics shows that the average person changes jobs nearly twelve times in their career and quite possibly not all of those changes will be their choice. Please believe me when I say, this doesn't have to be one of the most stressful experiences of your life if you treat it like the major Power Move it is.

I was once at a recruiting fair at the South by Southwest conference where candidates would approach our hiring booth and ask, "Hey! What's your company looking for?" My colleague and I would respond at the same time, "Well, what are *you* looking for? Perhaps we have a role open." I can't remember what we were really thinking, but when you know what you want, it makes the process not only better and easier for you, but it also makes it better for everyone else (i.e., a future employer!). Knowing what you want is *important*. Otherwise, anything will work.

In today's crowded, hypercompetitive, time-urgent digital landscape, any uncertainty about what you want is likely to hurt your cause. If you don't know what you want to do, or exactly what your skills and knowledge would qualify you to do, then please make the appropriate Power Move and take the time to find out.

Just as important—whether you're looking for a new job or a different position in your current company, you need to get your head in the right place. Stay clear of common career traps and try to see things from the perspective of your future employer. This means be realistic.

If the position calls for a graphic artist and you've never designed a thing, you're not being realistic—unless, of course, you're prepared to acquire the necessary skills and experience before you apply. A poor fit today doesn't necessarily mean it's a poor fit in the future, if you change. Never sell yourself short but consider how an employer will think given the circumstances when you apply. It's all about the fit of your skills and values with the needs and culture of a future employer.

When it comes to a job search, there are some habits that will provide a clear advantage:

1. **Treat career hunting like a job—even if it's a part-time one:** Let's assume you've determined your company matches for a new job. Now what? Time to tailor your application materials like résumé and cover letter, update your LinkedIn, polish your personal brand, start following your company matches online, and get to know the company better. Maybe they have events you can attend, employees you can network with, or volunteer opportunities that need your support. Whatever it is, engagement is required, and it's required like it is its own job. Create some structure for your career hunt by scheduling dedicated time each day or week to make progress. Creating structure for

your career hunt progress will also protect you from burnout, anxiety, or even that inner critic. Power habits like these also create space for you to recharge—both physically and mentally.

2. **Get curious, start learning:** What knowledge do you want to acquire right now? What are some skills or interests that appeal to and excite you, even if—and especially if—your current work isn't providing them? The adage from preschool remains true: we can't possibly know if we'll enjoy something if we've never tried it. So, even if you're SURE a particular type of work isn't a fit (e.g., you've always been a creative and are up for a job in marketing), it may still be worth giving it a go if the circumstances surrounding it are right.

Research shows that humans are notoriously bad at knowing what will actually make us happy, a phenomenon that only intensifies as we get older and our ideas about how life "should" be become more fixed. But I encourage you to tear away your resistance, flip your beliefs about yourself and what you like on their heads, and start exploring a wide range of possibilities—including careers and positions you've rejected in the past and things you've never thought of before. Why? Because obtaining diverse experience and skills makes us stronger candidates, enabling us to be more innovative and creative and even expand the longevity of our careers. And learning new things will keep you engaged, with your head in the game. Online learning is a convenient option with classes on Career Contessa, Skillshare, and LinkedIn Learning, but there are also skill-specific schools like Codecademy, IDEO U, and CreativeLive. You can also attend in-person classes at universities, community colleges, and General Assembly, and look for local workshops in your cities. Do not be afraid to consider relevant side hustles, short-term projects, and even full-on careers you may have rejected in the past—who doesn't want more skills and inspiration to pull from?

3. **Remember you're more than your career:** A big part of the myth of the dream job is the pressure we put on ourselves to get everything "right," make the "right" decisions, find the "right" jobs, be "right." This line of thinking—and the anxiety surrounding it—strongly suggests that there is some terrifying wrong path, that there are wrong decisions, that ultimately, you yourself will go wrong. None of this is true. First, you are not a fixed point, you're part of a process that will continue as long as you live. There will be ups and downs, sideways detours and remarkable shortcuts. The greatest wisdom I can pass on to you is to not let your identity be your career. Keep a big part of yourself (and what you like about yourself) separate and not defined by your work.

When you're looking for work, your attitude is huge. I'm sure I don't need to explain, but confidence sells itself. So you must realize that mistakes and failure are part of life. It will never be perfect. It might be challenging at first but learn to accept the fact that your so-called mistakes are as important to discovering who you are and what you want as your successes. Not knowing what you're going to do or if what you're doing is "right" is part of the process. Remind yourself again and again that work is just work and you are 100 percent okay with your ever-evolving career path. A career is meant to help support your life, not to become you.

Here are some other things you can do—not always easy, I know—that qualify as Power Moves in our book:

- Stop tormenting yourself with the idea that a job is supposed to be amazing all the time or else you have failed.

- Learn to accept the negative aspects in the career (or careers) you choose. Of course, this can be challenging. You may find that, depending on your personal circumstances, there may be times when any and all work is disappointing and unsatisfying. If you begin to look at the bad times as opportunities to learn instead of failures and stop judging yourself for what you did wrong, you will begin to value every part of the process instead of making yourself feel bad—which is never a good idea. A gentle reminder that your self-worth is too important to jeopardize for anyone or anything.
- Know that what you're actually looking for is a simple calculation: it's the intersection between what you're good at, what gives you energy, and what will pay you. Start zeroing in on that.

Get Social with It

No matter where you are in your career—senior, junior, freelance, anything in between—you need to be communicating with other people (and hopefully diverse groups of people who live and work in places different from you) as often as you can. Anyone can make this Power Move, which pays dividends for life—and never bigger than when you're looking for a job.

One of the best Power Moves I've ever made was engaging in informational interviews/nonnetworking, getting to know women I admire and asking them for advice and insights about things I'm fascinated by and interested in. Informational interviews are inherently social; they not only give you information, they give you connection, help you begin to build structures of community, and usually leave you feeling less untethered than you did before.

Going social is particularly important when you're looking for a job. For more than just financial reasons, unemployment can be tough—loneliness and depression are contagious. So even if you are not going to conduct informational interviews, make sure you are creating support through online communities, activities with friends and family, or even joining group fitness classes. Some socialization each week, especially if you're unemployed or work remotely the majority of the time, is a necessity. Socializing helps you not only feel professionally connected; it reaffirms your identity in things outside of your work.

I Don't Want to Leave, Just Progress

Sometimes your search is internal. Parts of your work life are sufficiently good for you to want to stay. Whatever they are, you still want more—whether it's a new challenge, an opportunity to expand your skills, or even a different work team. Since most companies favor internal hires, you already have an advantage.

Get specific with what you want. Identify how your current position doesn't align with what you want and need. Be honest about what's causing you to think this way. Is it because you want something different, or are you unhappy with your work responsibilities, colleagues, boss, etc.? Do your skills need to be expanded? Are you willing to take a position of lower pay or title? Are you a fit with any openings? Will you have the support of your boss? These are only a few of the questions you'll need to ask and answer. And, remember:

- You can let go of the idea of a "dream job," because it doesn't even exist.

- Our dreams are never about just one job or destination—the best careers adapt to our changing work-life needs and keep us excited and engaged.
- The perfect job when you're in your twenties will most likely be totally different to you when you're in your thirties, forties, and beyond; the dream will change and morph, expand and shrink over the course of your working life, and that's a really good thing.
- Instead of fixating on the goal of an elusive "dream job," start proactively taking practical, concrete steps to find the job you want right now.
- By focusing on taking small steps each day that add up to bigger steps, you're more likely to meet your goals and have more fun during the process overall.

Looking for a new job is serious work. It takes time, thought, and preparation, like any other job. The most successful searches benefit from decisions made well in advance. Knowing that your career is likely to experience change, you have the opportunity to take control of your career now, to adopt a Power Moves approach and have the career you want, on your terms.

DON'T FORGET MONEY

It's nearly impossible to hear the words "career success and fulfillment" and not think about money. It's likely that all of us (at some point) have used money as a measure of our career success and fulfillment. I'm not here to tell you this is wrong, but you really do need to be aware of how it can affect your thinking, and how to have a proactive and realistic relationship with money so you can build a fulfilling career on your terms. There's little doubt when it comes to earning and managing money that a lack of this resource can limit your career flexibility and critically impair your ability to make a Power Move.

Women have made amazing strides in just a few short decades (to wit: we weren't even legally permitted to have our own credit cards until 1974!). The good news is that we're leading the charge in graduation rates, launching twice as many new businesses as our male counterparts, and sitting in more C-suites than ever before (but still not enough!).

Yet many women, including many successful women, continue to struggle with money in concerning ways: from the things that are less in women's control, like the wage gap and the pink tax, to a lack of financial confidence overall. Women's issues with money also stem from irresponsible messaging that says how much we make defines who we are, that it's somehow a key indicator of our worth. The link between your salary and your feelings of success has been hardwired into your brain—thanks mostly to incessantly being asked to "know your worth," "ask for your worth," "demand your worth" in every salary negotiation advice article or video you've ever seen.

However you deal with money and all that it involves, the tools described in this section will provide a basic awareness, enabling you to make the Power Moves right for you. For sure, money has a unique relationship with Power Moves. It can directly affect your ability to make Power Moves, and, alternatively, Power Moves can directly affect your earnings and net worth. This is why you need to know these tools.

CHAPTER 23

Your Relationship with Money

Money is obviously a complicated issue—and it can be difficult to divorce our inherent bias about money and our emotional reactions surrounding it from what it really is. At its core, money is power, it is safety, it allows you freedom and independence and even influence. Money is foundational; having enough of it can give you a sense of stability and security like almost nothing else in your life ever will. Without enough money, you can feel trapped and afraid. The fear over not making rent or meeting your or your family's basic needs leads to anxiety that can take over your entire life. That's why you want to be smart and strategic about money—to know how much you need to earn to live the life you want, to manage the money you bring in, to plan and prepare yourself for a secure financial future.

But money and our thoughts around money can be dangerous when we attach too much value to it, when we wrap up our self-worth in an arbitrary salary number, when we make money the entire focus of our lives. For many of us, myself included, your amount of income might also be a measure of your self-worth. If you have a high salary, you might think it also means you have a higher status. And if your salary is lower than someone in your circle (like a spouse), you might think you need to compensate in other ways because you feel inadequate. Regardless of where your income level stands, I know for certain that you're building a really shaky foundation for life when you intertwine your identity with your compensation.

Your relationship with money—like your relationship with anything—should be balanced and thoughtful and constantly evolving. Your money needs today may look far different from what you'll need in five years, ten years, and more. Money can be a well of deep satisfaction; earning enough will be a source of pride, but obsessing over it, tying up your self-worth in it, can be a dangerous game with a shallow reward.

Stop Believing Your Self-Worth Is Your Net Worth

Put an end to the thinking that your worth is tied up in the amount of money you make and stop using the kind of language that surrounds it. Here are some steps to combat this thinking:

1. Find examples in your life that are not related to money that make you feel good about yourself. Share those moments with friends and family, and even write them down. The goal is to start associating your self-worth with feelings and experiences that deserve it and have nothing to do with your bank accounts.
2. Once you identify experiences that support your new mind-set, seek out related opportunities that you can practice frequently.

For example, if volunteering your time helps you shift your mind-set, seek out more volunteer opportunities.

3. Spend time with people whose views on money support your new mind-set. Ditch the materialistic friend who's always talking about how much money she makes or flaunting her newest on-line order.

4. Create a healthy money mantra. Feel free to use mine: "My self-worth does not equal my net worth." Say this to yourself again and again, particularly around times of financial anxiety or shame.

Not only is connecting your self-worth to your net worth a losing game, it also throws a huge wrench into this whole self-acceptance thing we're going for; it's a distraction, and yet another thing that disrupts your power and limits your ability to make smart, customized, unconventional decisions about where you want to go next professionally.

Shifting your mind-set will not be easy—but in the long term, your mental, physical, and emotional health with thank you pro-fusely. Start thinking about money in less insecure, more empowered ways that enable Power Moves.

CHAPTER 24

Let Go of Your Fear of Money— for Good

There's a lot of evidence to support the fact that women have more fears, anxiety, and blocks surrounding money than men. No surprise, really, since not that long ago women couldn't even have their own bank accounts. These challenges often manifest from not being sufficiently educated about money when we were young, and they revolve around just a few basic areas:

- feeling "stupid" about money or that we don't "deserve" it
- fear of using credit and long-term debt
- shame about having an abundance of money
- planning for the future (e.g., a family, a house)
- fear of taking risks and/or investing (leading to the so-called investment gap)
- feeling intimidated by the power of money

- not saving enough for retirement
- fear of losing a job or full-on financial ruin

You're worried that you don't know enough about money, that you are unworthy of it, that if you take risks with it, you will fail. The entire idea of appropriate savings plans and long-term financial planning can seem overwhelming, a drag, a task that's doomed to failure, and so some of us shut down. This puts us at a distinct disadvantage: money should be empowering, a means to gain security and control. Ignoring our finances leaves us more insecure and unstable—it's a vicious circle: you're afraid of being foolish with money and you don't pay enough attention to it, don't ask for what you deserve, don't plan or organize well enough, make poor decisions, and, ultimately, become the money fool you were afraid to be in the first place.

Remember that only YOU are responsible for making your money work for you. Not your company. Not your boss. When you're young, you can grow accustomed to having a person (coach, parent, teacher) keep you accountable and guide you through adult decisions. But by the time you get your first job, it's definitely time to take control of your bank accounts, for *you* and *your* future. An added bonus? Being in control (and aware) of your money will inevitably bring you an inner calm. Never fear even if you haven't started yet! There are simple, straightforward ways to educate yourself and start feeling confident about money ASAP. I'm listing some essential steps below, but when you are ready to get serious about your money, you should consult a financial planner to be fully versed on how to personalize your plan for the future. Now that's a Power Move.

Identify Your Money Fears and Start Addressing Them

I'll bet you didn't know chrometophobia is the intense fear of money. It indicates a deep aversion, dread, or fear around all financial things, and it's surprisingly common. Your panic about money may not be quite this extreme; you may feel merely uncomfortable talking about money or asking for it. You may not understand your market value and feel shaky and timid about how to ask for a raise or set a rate for your services or a salary requirement. Everyone is anxious about money sometimes, but if this fear is prohibiting you from earning all you can and should, when it's literally impacting your bottom line, it's vital that you start addressing this behavior.

Money can feel emotional, personal, and intimate. It can trigger class issues, complicate relationships, reflect our identity and sense of self in both positive and definitely not so positive ways. What's often overlooked is how our relationship with and emotional attachment to money is a strong indicator of how we'll handle our finances; without sorting out where there are conflicts or issues, we will most likely continue to make the same mistakes. In fact, financial powerhouse Suze Orman says that women's money struggles are a strong reflection of other problems in our lives—in our personal relationships or feelings of self-worth. Work on those issues, she believes, and the money problems may begin to fall away.

To start, if you're not pleased with where you are financially, identify what motivates you when it comes to money and what's getting in your way—what are the emotional stumbling blocks that are keeping you from financial freedom?

For example, if you're afraid of what will happen if you ask for a raise, start examining the source of this fear. Are you afraid you'll be fired? Do you wonder if you actually deserve this raise? Assess your position and accomplishments in your current job. Anchor yourself in reality and get out of your head and your impostor feelings. Look back at your past performance reviews and take an inventory of your work over the past year. If you feel there are areas you could improve, begin to improve them, but set a timeline and make a commitment (and stick to it) to a date when you'll request a raise. By being proactive and consistently following through with plans, we begin to become accustomed to asking for and receiving what we deserve.

Another money challenge that can lead to fear is feeling intimidated by money terminology! Not knowing where to begin because there's a lack of understanding around money words can naturally keep you from starting to talk about money. The glossary on the following page is by no means comprehensive—but it's a start. Remember that almost everything feels insurmountable in the beginning and seek out supportive financial advisers you trust and can be honest with—never hire someone who condescends to you or makes you feel foolish or small. The opposite of a Power Move!

How to Honestly Assess Your Financial Picture

One of the biggest impediments to women's economic success is being afraid to look at our finances honestly and directly—instead, we feel overwhelmed by the numbers or too scared to know how truly bad it might be. And so some stay in denial, living above their means, not saving, getting further into debt, and hiding from it all. But I am here to tell you: ignoring your money will not make anything better; it will only exacerbate the problem. Staying in the dark about your money is far scarier than pulling together a few statements and creating a spreadsheet. And even if you look at the full picture and find it grim, it is so much better for not only your finances but also your psyche to start living in financial reality as soon as you can.

Financial Glossary

Liquidity	Measures how quickly and easily you can convert different financial assets into cash. Cash, savings, and checking accounts are considered the most "liquid," while CDs, stocks, and mutual funds are harder to change to usable funds.
Portfolio	This has nothing to do with art or creative work. In finance, your portfolio is your assets: Your savings, your bonds, your stocks. Ideally this is multiple financial assets with varying levels of risk.
Pension	A plan requires employers to contribute to a fund for your retirement. The company invests that money into stocks and bonds, and the earnings become your salary once you retire. Most companies also allow workers to contribute part of their own income to their pension fund, typically via a 401(k) or a 403(b) plan.
Broker	So you don't have the time or know-how to suss out and sell stocks on top of, you know, your real job. Brokers are people and businesses who, for a fee, will do the dirty work for you. Discount brokers will buy and sell orders that you place online for around $5-15 per transaction. Full-service brokers offer more advice on retirement planning and investing, but they'll charge a higher commission for it.
Principle	The initial money you put into an investment.
Compound Interest	With compounding interest, you'll collect interest on both your principle and any previous interest you've earned. By saving money, you're making money. The average interest rate on the stock market since 1929 has been around 7-8%. If you earn the same average return of 7 percent on your investments over the next 20 to 30 years, plus compounding, you're setting yourself up for a much more comfortable retirement.
Net Worth	Net worth is a simple calculation of a company's total tangible assets (basically everything but copyrights, patents, and intellectual property) minus the company's debt.

Income Statement	Consider this a report card for your investments. The income statement will provide some information about the company's performance (over a specific time period) that affects its stock price, including its sales and earnings per share. Consult statements to select and evaluate your stocks.
Capital + Capital Appreciation	If you're investing in a company, you also need to guess how it's going to perform next year—and the year after that. As we've seen often, even the most profitable companies can fail quickly if they generate a PR controversies or a competitor beats them to a new technology. Capital signals a company's future strength, measuring both its revenue and the people, technologies, and tools it can use to gain more revenue later on. If a company has more capital, more people will invest in it and its stock price will rise. So when companies use their profits to improve their products or the company itself, they'll increase their capital and their stock price. When that happens? Your stock is now worth more (i.e., the capital has appreciated), and you can sell it for a profit.
Dividends	Other companies will share their profits directly with stockholders in the form of a dividend (either with money or more stocks).
Mutal Fund	You can't afford a studio in your favorite neighborhood, so you and your friends find a three-bedroom apartment there and split the rent. Mutual funds work the same way, except that you and other people pool your money to make larger investments than you could alone. Money managers will invest it, and your group will receive the ultimate earnings (or losses). But because you're holding professionally managed stocks in a range of industries, mutual funds are typically less risky than individual stocks.
Passive Income	This is consistent money one earns no matter if they are actively working or not — for example, rental income.
Maturity Date	The date that the CD expires and you get your money plus interest.
401 (k)	A 401(K) is an employer-sponsored retirement plan that you can contribute to directly and automatically, from your paycheck. You won't have to pay taxes on it until you withdraw it (starting at age 59 ½ without penalty for all retirement plans). Many employers will also match your contributions up to a certain percentage, which means free money.

403 (b)	Essentially a 401(k) for employees of nonprofits.
529 Plan	A 529 plan is a college savings plan, which some employers now offer alongside retirement plans. Like 401(k)s and 403(b)s, you can contribute to 529s straight from your pre-tax income. In several states, you can use a pre-paid tuition plan to pre-pay future tuition costs at participating colleges. If your state doesn't offer a pre-paid option, choose a 529 savings plan, which invests in stocks and bonds. As long as you spend your earnings on qualified college expenses (typically only tuition), they won't be subject to federal or state taxes.
Defined Benefit Plans & Defined Contribution Plans	Twist! These are essentially the same as 401(k)s.
Traditional IRA vs. Roth IRA	The difference between them comes down to taxes. For a Traditional IRA, you won't be taxed on any of your contributions now, but you'll have to pay taxes on your withdrawals in retirement. With a Roth IRA, you'll pay taxes on your contributions now so you can skip them once you're retired. To choose between the two, compare your current income with what you hope to make on a fixed income when you retire. Choose a Roth if you're currently earning under $118,000 per year ($186,000 for married couples), but plan to make more in retirement. If you're rolling in cash now and cutting back in retirement, pick a traditional.
Financial Plan	A financial plan captures your financial goals and targets, and establishes how you plan to achieve them. Identifying your goals and making a plan increases the likelihood that you'll achieve what you've set out to achieve. A typical financial plan helps you envision the future by capturing your income, savings and investing activities in pursuit of your goals—whether that's building an emergency fund, saving up to buy a house or investing towards your future.
Financial Advisor	The biggest thing to point out here is that "financial adviser" can mean lots of different things, and there's no hard and fast rule for who can call him or herself one. Basically, a financial adviser is someone who can give you advice on your money, sometimes including investing. The key here is to do your research about their backgrounds. There are also services online that offer digital era financial advisers.
APR	Annual Percentage Rate, which means the yearly rate you'll be charged for borrowing money.
APV	The adjusted present value is the net present value of a project or company if financed solely by equity plus the present value of any financing benefits, which are the additional effects of debt.
The Vanguard Group	This is the largest provider of mutual funds (IRAs, 401ks) in the world with more than $5 trillion dollars in assets.

Understanding your financial outlook in a raw and honest way will enable you to make smarter decisions, to start feeling more secure and in control. It will help you decide if you really need to stay in this job you hate, or if you can take a risk doing something you love. Denial is the enemy of true safety and security. Knowledge is, as they say, power. It can be liberating as hell too. So don't delay! Start by making friends with your debt:

- Identify all the balances from all of your accounts.
- Check interest rates on each credit card.
- Check your credit score and credit analysis—are there collections you don't know about? Accounts you've forgotten?
- Research if you may be able to reduce payments with a better interest rate on a different card or a debt consolidation plan.
- Spend time planning how long it will take you to pay off your balances and develop a plan to do so. (Pro tip: start with paying off your high-interest credit cards!)
- Begin this month by vowing not to spend more than you make.

Really Track Your Spending

You need more savings. We all do. In a 2018 survey, Bankrate.com found that fifty-five million Americans have zero dollars put away for an emergency and 61 percent of all Americans have less than one thousand dollars. Your first step to saving is understanding where your money is going. Set yourself up with a budget tracking system like Mint to see exactly what you spend and where (there are few things more sobering than realizing you spent thousands of dollars on takeout and parking over the course of a year).

After you have a handle on what you spend, commit to a small savings plan. Even if it's fifty dollars a month. Direct your bank to transfer that money automatically into a savings account on payday, before you even have a chance to see it. Financial expert Amanda Holden recommends having six months of living expenses saved in the event of a layoff or emergency. You'll also want to make sure you're maximizing your benefits at work. Ashley Feinstein Gerstley of The Fiscal Femme has this to say about benefits:

> When we start out at any new company, we often get a lot of information about our benefits as we are trying to hit the ground running in our new jobs. Our benefits can become an afterthought, but they are a very important part of our total compensation. Schedule some time in the calendar to look at what's offered and make sure to maximize the things that are beneficial to you—especially your 401(k).
>
> One of the most important benefits (after healthcare!) is our 401(k). Many companies offer 401(k) match which is free additional money when you contribute (up to a certain amount). Even if your company doesn't offer 401(k) matching, there are tax benefits to contributing to a 401(k) that make it worth it!

Once you've started to take these steps—and you're feeling less scared because you are armed with information and beginning to solve your money mystery—commit to a budget. Find a budgeting app or try the Career Contessa budgeting worksheet (below). Remember: budgeting is not boring. Budgeting is empowering. Budgeting puts you in control. Budgeting is adult, and being a full, in-charge adult is one of the smartest self-care things you can practice.

The career contessa **Budgeting Tool**

Take control of your spending with this financial calculator:

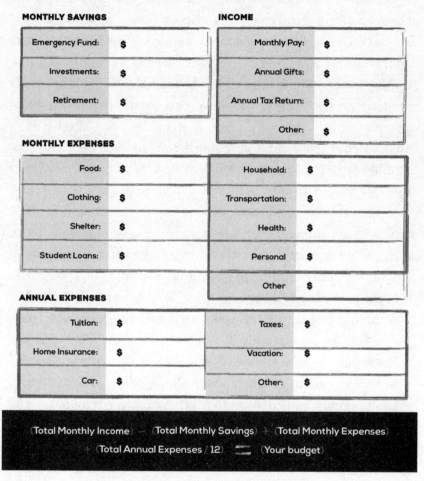

MONTHLY SAVINGS

Emergency Fund:	$
Investments:	$
Retirement:	$

INCOME

Monthly Pay:	$
Annual Gifts:	$
Annual Tax Return:	$
Other:	$

MONTHLY EXPENSES

Food:	$	Household:	$
Clothing:	$	Transportation:	$
Shelter:	$	Health:	$
Student Loans:	$	Personal	$
		Other	$

ANNUAL EXPENSES

Tuition:	$	Taxes:	$
Home Insurance:	$	Vacation:	$
Car:	$	Other:	$

(Total Monthly Income) − (Total Monthly Savings) + (Total Monthly Expenses) + (Total Annual Expenses / 12) ⟶ (Your budget)

Closing Your Own Money Gap

There might come times in your life when, in order to make a Power Move, get what you want longer term, or go after a goal—like becoming debt-free, gaining more education or skills, or pivoting into a new professional direction—you may need to supplement your nine-to-five (or five-to-nine) income. Side hustles can be an incredible way to build your confidence, and picking up extra money can give you freedom to explore new opportunities and fast-track your goals. For example, perhaps having a bit of extra money allows you to make the Power Move of attending that networking event and buying a glass of wine, instead of skipping the event altogether because you're worried about what a ten-dollar expense means. Or maybe a side hustle gives you the security to build an emergency fund more quickly. Whatever the reason for needing extra money, there are four key things I tell all Career Contessa readers to keep in mind when we're discussing side jobs:

1. Never, ever work on your side hustle during regular work hours.
2. Never allow your side hustle to negatively affect the quality of your work or commitment to your "day" job.
3. Make sure your full-time contract does not prohibit you from doing work on the side. If you have a noncompete clause, make sure you are not violating it.
4. Make your health a priority, and do not run yourself ragged. Be diligent about getting enough sleep, eating well, hydrating, seeing family and friends. Your physical and emotional health always come first.

Once you know you can follow the above rules, it's time to explore side hustles that support your goals—both financially and professionally.

CHAPTER 25

Know Your Work Value

Do you know the value of your work? No matter their financial wealth, no matter their situation, everyone wants to be paid fairly for their efforts. Receiving compensation in line with what value you/your skills bring to work is the most basic money principle. The problem isn't the concept, it's first determining what your work value is, and then getting paid for that value.

In the workplace, your work value is determined by what an employer will pay you. Or, if you're an entrepreneur, what your customers will pay for your goods or services or intellectual efforts. Unfortunately, your work is not valued at a million dollars—unless someone (or some company) will pay you that amount. Ego has a way of confusing things, particularly when we think we are "worth" more than we are being paid, but at the end of the day, your work value is really set by what others—the market—will pay you.

So, what's that number? Obviously, it depends on a lot of factors—like your education, skills, experience, interpersonal skills (i.e., ability to work with/communicate with others), growth potential, flexibility, and much more. For most of us, the best way to determine what our unique bundle of talent, knowledge, and experience is valued at is to identify what others with a similar bundle are being paid.

Unfortunately, it can be hard to find comparative pay information. It's not often that you hear two friends talk openly about their finances, and two colleagues discussing their salaries and benefits openly is basically a nonstarter. In fact, most of us were taught to keep quiet when it comes to money. According to a recent Bustle survey, 50 percent of people said they never discuss personal finances with friends.

We come by our attitudes about money honestly too. Many of us didn't have parents talking openly about salaries, and we probably received the message that talking about it was taboo, or worse—our employers have a "rule" that doesn't allow it. I know this was the case for me. I once worked for a company that told me I would be in "danger" of being let go if I shared my salary information with my colleagues. Now, of course, I know that's not even legal.

It's time to change this behavior. We need to stop looking at money as a bad topic and start looking at it as a power topic—starting with salary transparency. Salary awareness can help ensure that there is wage equality for equal work. It can also make us more comfortable asking for more money when we know we deserve it. Salary transparency can lead to more awareness of other workplace issues and build trust. For example, transparency about harassment, discrimination, and unconscious bias are clear benefits. Side note—women and minorities are the most affected by these workplace issues!

As I write this book in 2019, only a small percentage of companies have adopted pay transparency practices, even with a growing demand from employees, which means it's up to you to start the conversations—and even influence your company to start more open communication about compensation. For starters, communication about the company's compensation practices means employees will have a clearer understanding of the compensation philosophy and objectives. Clarity involves understanding what compensation data the company uses to create base salaries, and how things like experience and performance weigh in. It's communicating how bonuses and raises are structured—and when those happen. The company might also need to explain what type of labor market they are competing in. For example, the need for experienced technical talent might require the company to pay more than market rates to compete with the companies around them.

Every company's level of transparency will be different, but the goal is to get companies to start thinking about *some* level of transparency. Transparency builds trust in your organization, which can lead to employee engagement and retention. Countless studies have proved that engaged employees lead to better business outcomes. PayScale conducted a survey and found "that one of the top predictors of employee sentiment, including 'satisfaction' and 'intent to leave,' was a company's ability to communicate clearly about compensation. In fact, open and honest discussion around pay was found to be more important than typical measures of employee engagement, such as career advancement opportunities, employer appreciation, and future enthusiasm for the company."

If salary transparency is not something your company is currently communicating, you can start the conversation with your manager, your HR/recruitment teams, and even your colleagues.

Understand that sharing information about work compensation doesn't make you nosy or vindictive—it makes you an engaged employee who would rather know that you're being paid fairly for your skills than live in the unknown. Frankly, transparency is good for business and good for you.

Once you're committed to being more transparent about your salary information, it's time to start sharing. You can tiptoe into this with online salary databases—Career Contessa's database, The Salary Project™, is even anonymous!—and then move forward with directly asking your colleagues how much they make. I know that idea probably made you cringe, but it's necessary to know what your peers are making to determine if you're being paid fairly for your work value.

I recommend doing this in person (i.e., not over text, email, etc.) and in a private space—maybe even outside of the office. Your goal is not only to learn their compensation but also to gain a solid understanding of their role. For example, let's say you're a property manager, and you manage ten properties. Your colleague is also a property manager, and they manage five properties. On paper, it looks like you're doing double the work, but as you ask more questions, you realize that both of you manage the same number of tenants with about equal work and bring in similar revenue for the company. This information is helpful because now when you share salary information you have a realistic basis for comparison.

Also, remember that salary is usually just one part of your compensation package. What about bonuses? What about other benefits? Consider expanding your questions beyond salary so you're operating with the full picture of information. As you do collect information, keep track of it so it can become your own personal salary project.

As you get more comfortable, you can reach out to peers at other companies or within similar industries and ask them directly what their salary is. I always find it helpful to provide context to your request with something like, "I'm researching the market value for X role across different companies. Your salary information will really help with that research—would you be willing to share? I'm happy to share my salary number as well." Some people will not be comfortable with this, and that's okay! Go to the next person—and then the next.

If you're an entrepreneur, freelancer, or working in a job where you're typically paid per project, client, etc., you should also consider asking similarly employed peers what they make, with an understanding about their work, deliverables, results, etc. I was once at a marketing breakfast with a handful of brand managers who were talking about hiring influencers to promote their products. Shockingly, some of these managers bragged about the fact that they paid some influencers less than others because they had no idea what the market rate was. This wake-up call inspired me to start a whisper network—an idea I heard about from Ask For It founder Alexandra Dickinson. The concept is pretty simple. It's a secret group of people who share the ins and outs of their compensation or pay rates. The groups are usually invite-only, and the common theme is that the members work in a similar field or with similar companies. Whisper networks are a great way to make sure you're paid fairly, because even if none of the members of your group have worked with a particular company before, they might have suggestions for what you should charge.

Last, if you're conducting salary research because you want to ask for a raise, you'll just swap out some of the wording in my earlier example to "I'm preparing to ask for a raise, and I'm researching the market value for my skill set, as well as how raises have been structured for other employees here." Your research will help you get a better understanding on how your company handles raises in general, and that can be extremely beneficial as you start to prepare to ask for a raise.

Let's review some steps you can take to determine your number, whether you're applying for a job or gunning for a raise. And because I don't want to be biased in just suggesting what's worked for the Career Contessa team, I've also tapped Kate Westervelt, founder of MOMBOX and alum of companies like Wayfair, *Good Housekeeping*, the *Financial Times*, and more, to offer her insight.

1. **Research—and then do more research:** Scour the web for company review websites (think Glassdoor.com, InHerSight.com, etc.) and look at comparable titles within the company. Then look at the cross-market salaries of people similarly situated in the industry. Use salary research tools like The Salary Project™ at Career Contessa to look at salary data across industries, job titles, and years of experience. Keep in mind that location is often a major factor in salary. Big-city roles can usually command higher salaries because the applicant pool and cost of living are generally much higher. Also note how unique the role is—is this a common position where many people do the same work? If so, there's probably less salary wiggle room than, say, a specialized position. Next, evaluate how far you moved the needle at your current job. Make a bullet list of the things you've accomplished and compare those to your original job description. Have you exceeded expectations? If your results are tied to actual company revenue, have those hard numbers handy as well. This is where you'll humbly explain how talented you are and how your track record proves it. Not that experienced yet? Be sure you're fairly assessing the work you've actually done instead of what you think you're capable of doing someday. We know how tough a low salary can be, but keep in mind, you have the rest of your working life to hit your salary goal! Right now, focus on hard work, learning, and genuine networking.

2. **Talk to real people:** Salary negotiation expert Alexandra Dickinson recommends connecting with five to six people (both men and women, since men are, on average, paid 20 percent more than women for the same job!) in your industry and job function—

even better if you know someone who works at the company you're applying to!—and ask them what their salaries are. Remember, you can soften "the ask" by providing context. Tell them that you're applying for a new job and while you've conducted research that shows you should ask for something in the range of X and Y, you'd really appreciate their feedback on what they think of that range. Or you can ask directly what they make, following the advice mentioned earlier in this chapter. If you don't know anyone in the industry or job function you're applying for, you can send an email to people in your network to see if they can make any introductions. Something like this would work:

> *Hi Name,*
>
> *I'm working on collecting some salary research for a new role I'm applying for, and I noticed you're connected to XYZ person in a similar role. I'd love to learn more about their role and salary to see if my research holds up in real life.*
>   *Would you be able to make an introduction for me?*
>
> *Best,*
> *Name*

3. **Self-evaluate:** If it applies, consider all the amazing results and contributions you've made with your current company. Where have you gone above and beyond? What are the hard numbers that back up how you've benefited your current employer? You'll want to be able to share specific stories and results of your work, so take time to reflect before you determine your number.

4. **Be forward-thinking:** In addition to thinking about what you've done so far in your career, consider how you'll add value to your current (or new) employer. Why should they pay you X? How can you paint a very impressive picture of the impact you'll make? Impressive employees (and candidates) who are confident about what they can offer an organization will have more opportunity to ask for—and get—the top of their salary range.

5. **Develop a range:** There's no one number that describes your work value to every possible employer, in every possible environment. The fact is, your value can vary simply because employers are not all the same. So always make it a practice of developing a pay range and understand the biggest factors that affect your range. For example, a well-funded start-up might pay more for the same role than an established company with an active training program.

When in Doubt, Use This Salary Equation

Determining your own salary requirements—which we know can be different from value—can feel like an insurmountable task, especially if you're in a newer field or a groundbreaking role. At Career Contessa, we had a reader reach out to us with this impossible question.

This reader was offered a new full-time position at a company where she was interning. Awesome news, right? Well, it was—right up until they told her to name her salary. Upon offering the position, her new manager flippantly said, "Name what you think is reasonable."

This reader reached out to us asking, "How do I figure out a good number?"

By that time, Career Contessa had been around for a few years. And yet. This question really stumped us. Here's the thing. Salary *is* pretty subjective, and it relies on a ton of variables—the industry, the location, your experiences, the company itself, and, frankly, the company's cash flow.

What we couldn't believe was that there seemed to be no equation for creating a good, fair, earned salary. We searched high and low for an answer, because we needed it—and fast. Our entire team brought the question home to our partners, we called our peers, and we even posed the question over LinkedIn. How do you determine a fair salary—no matter who you are?

We were fortunate enough to connect with someone who just happens to work for a company that funds women-run start-up ventures in San Francisco. That unanswerable question about how to determine a salary for person X in city Y with Z years of experience? This woman *owned* it. Even better? She shared it with us:

1. **Add up your monthly expenses:** "This is a fun job," said nobody ever. Pull up your monthly statements for the past ninety days and add every item. Tally up what you spend on necessities and recurring bills—the expenses you have every month.

   Necessities: rent, mortgage, health insurance.
   Recurring bills: gas, cell phone bill, groceries, etc.

   These are your real expenses. They don't include that fancy dinner you took your mom out to (she always deserves it, anyway), and they don't include the elaborate bachelorette weekend you had to attend. Your monthly expenses are those hard expenses you can expect to pay every month. Basically, it's the most un-fun money you spend.

2. **Double it:** Now that you've determined your monthly recurring expenses, double it. We all probably had a time in our lives when we lived paycheck to paycheck, spending every red penny before counting down to the next payday ("It's really five *more* days away?"). So double that first number. This gives you space for those incidentals, for the endless weddings you'll have to attend, and for savings. Yes, you should be building savings.

3. **Add 20 percent:** The next thing you'll do is add 20 percent to the number above. Get out your calculators and press Number x 1.20 = X. You'll multiply it by twelve to determine your yearly salary number.

Why?

For starters, you know that uncomfortable feeling you get when you're figuring out a salary? That voice in your head that begs, "Can I ask for that much?" Apply hard math to answer that question and assuage any doubt. Add 20 percent.

The 20 percent addition also gives you your buffer. Salary negotiation is just that—a negotiation. The company might come back with a lower number. If so, you've already padded your salary. This allows you both to land at a comfortable place. So there you have it. The not-so-secret salary sauce.

Determining a number—or, better yet, a range—is only the first step to obtaining your fair work value. This principle has a cousin, and that's the subject of the next Power Move tool—negotiating compensation that's a win for you and for your employer.

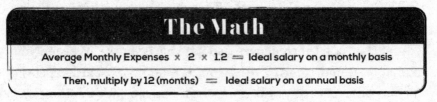

The Math

Average Monthly Expenses x 2 x 1.2 = Ideal salary on a monthly basis
Then, multiply by 12 (months) = Ideal salary on a annual basis

CHAPTER 26

Negotiate for Win-Win Success

Whether you're considering a new job, asking for that deserved raise, commanding a higher freelance rate, or stopping doing work for free, you need to make a habit of negotiating for your work value—an obvious Power Move. Once you've determined a fair pay range, it's time to make it happen. Pay negotiations can be stressful events, but remember, you're just asking for what you deserve in comparison to your work peers—based on the value you provide. There is absolutely nothing wrong with asking to be paid fairly.

Still, it's not easy for a lot of women to negotiate money issues. A recent study out of the University of Texas found that when women negotiate for themselves, they tend to ask for smaller salaries than men do or than they themselves do when they are advocating for others. The reason for this—beyond not knowing and general anxiety—is many women worry that when they ask for more money they'll be considered "pushy" and it will damage their image at work. And they may have some reason to be concerned: a 2017 study titled "Do Women Ask?" found that women actually do ask for raises as often as men, but we're more likely to be denied them or to receive blowback for speaking up about the subject in the first place (sending the message that it does in fact hurt to ask).

Let's take a look at two scenarios—negotiating for a raise and negotiating for compensation at a new job. Here's the process I recommend when you're negotiating with your employer for a raise.

How to Ask for a Raise

It's time to ask for a raise. Are you ready? I know, most people are terrified at the mere thought of asking for more money. But get this: asking for a raise can be incredibly motivating and empowering. Plus, taking the initiative to set up this meeting, arriving with a thoughtfully prepared case for yourself, and (hopefully) agreeing to that new salary is pretty much the ultimate Power Move of self-advocacy. Let's get started.

Before You Ask: Prepare, Prepare, Prepare

To be successful, there are two elements that must work in conjunction: preparation and timing.

Before you build your pitch for that raise we all know you deserve, you need the knowledge, data, and history to back up your ask. Also, you need to make sure the timing is correct. If your company is in the middle of working out a huge merger, maybe give it a minute. You don't want your amazing case to fall on distracted ears.

Do

- **Gather all of your praise:** Keep a file of all of those notes from clients, your boss, and your colleagues in which you were commended for a well-done job. This is a great "smile file" to have, regardless.
- **Go for raw data and real numbers:** Numbers don't lie. How has your company or department directly benefited from your work? Did your team play a role in increasing sales by X percent last year? Did you bring in X new clients? Is the team you oversee bigger than it was last year?
- **Plan your next steps:** You're asking for this raise because you've demonstrated that you'll go above and beyond, but your boss also wants to hear that you're in it for the long haul. How do you plan to continue growing within the company if you *do* get this raise?
- **What's in it for your boss?** I'm sure you've spent the last few months dreaming of how you could use a new salary—to build your savings or to finally move out of your studio apartment. But what does your boss get out of it? Would giving you the raise ensure that they have a stable person in a leadership role? Will your stepping up take work off of her back? These are things you should have in the back of your mind when formulating your big ask.
- **Present a hard number:** Ah yes, the most awkward part. Come prepared with a solid number, because they *will* ask for one. That number should be based on real research through conversations with peers in similar roles/industries and from online salary tools. Keep in mind that they're likely to counteroffer about 10–15 percent lower. Get started by identifying six peers (men and women) and ask if they'd be willing

to share their salary number with you so you can better understand what to ask for. If they aren't open to sharing their number, you can share the number or range you want to ask for and get their feedback on it.

Don't

- **Focus on the personal:** In fact, keep the personal out entirely. You deserve the raise because of your contributions, the change you've achieved, and the stellar work you will continue to do. It's as simple as that.
- **Ask at a terrible time:** The last thing you'll want to do is create a stunning case for your salary increase right in the middle of a hiring freeze. Keep an eye on what's going on in your company. When do they tend to hire new talent? Were others close to you recently promoted? Timing is everything, so do the work to make sure your timing is the best to your knowledge.
- **Present bloated numbers or take false credit:** Most projects are done as a team, and your boss knows too well what kind of work you've been doing. Don't say, "I've been working seventy-hour weeks," when we all know you haven't been. Or "I was responsible for increasing sales by 50 percent last year," when you worked with an entire team. Give credit where credit is due.

Some Other Tips

- **Get on the calendar:** You know when you're dying to have a conversation and you just pop into your boss's office? Don't do that in this case. But also don't wait for your annual review. Get yourself on the calendar. Schedule dedicated time to present and ask.

- **Don't just practice—record it:** This is a painful one, but so necessary. Make a quick recording of yourself pitching the raise ask. If you can, get a friend to sit with you. Practice makes perfect.

It's Time to Make the Ask

Every pitch, sale, or marketing effort is going to involve storytelling—good storytelling. What makes a good story? It's pretty simple—situation, conflict, and resolution. In your story, your resolution is you getting the raise.

The easiest way to do that is to cover the who, what, where, why, when, and how.

And now, Career Contessa's formula—"The GIMME":

G: Give Background Info
I: Introduce Why You're Awesome
M: Make Your Case Research-Based (This is where all that research comes in!)
M: Make the Ask
E: End with a Bang (Bang = how your future contributions will help the company!)

Let's recap: Asking for a raise is the ultimate self-advocacy. It's your right! And even your responsibility to yourself to make as much money as you can. Before you ask, be prepared. Find out comparable salaries, come in armed with reasons why it's time to give you this raise. And when you're still not sure, follow our formula for "raise-asking" along with considerations like the best time to ask, collecting your praise and accomplishments, etc., so when you do make that ask, it's impressive, you're impressive, and you get an impressive salary out of it.

Negotiating Compensation for a New Job

So how do you negotiate your pay for a new job? While the approach is similar to asking for a raise, there are a couple of notable differences. One of the questions you will probably get asked during the interview process is "What are your salary expectations?" This is often the first step in what can be a stressful process, particularly when you really want the position. Needless to say, there are differing opinions about the best way to negotiate and win your desired salary.

I'm not new to the question around salary expectations because when I was a recruiter at Hulu, it was the one question I always asked in my initial phone screens. However, before I share some steps you can follow for determining the number you provide in response, I want to explain why this question is being asked—and why it's great for you to name your salary number first. A lot of salary advice actually encourages you not to "throw out" the first number because they call that the "anchor number," which sets the tone for the rest of the negotiation. The general old-school advice is that you should delay stating your preferred salary range until you've made an offer *or* let the employer share their salary range first, but what happens if they offer something significantly lower?!

Our advice, and the advice we've heard from other women and seen work, is that you want to put out the first number (based on your research, of course), and that is a better strategy for being paid the market value for your skills. Here's how Inc.com puts it:

. . . some research has indicated that the result of a negotiation is often closer to what the first mover proposed than to the number the other party had in mind; the first number uttered in a negotiation (so long as it is not ridiculous) has the effect of "anchoring the conversation."

In other words, throwing out the first number gives you the opportunity to use what's called anchoring bias in your favor. Using the advice provided in the previous tool ("Know Your Work Value"), you've come prepared with a number or range following your thorough research. Here's what comes next:

Present your number or salary range. "Where do you want to be salary-wise?" the interviewer says so casually, you'd think she was asking if you'd like cream with your coffee.

Stay cool. This is where men and women tend to differ. Men often give a distinct number based off of market research and self-evaluation. Women tend to give a wishy-washy version of what they'd settle for. If you've done your market research and you've taken the time to validate what you bring to the table, state your requirements in a concrete fashion. Next, be prepared to explain why you feel this number is appropriate.

When the interviewer asks if this number is flexible, simply state you'd be able to reassess once you've seen the entire packaged offer. Keep in mind, your "package" could include anything from company equity, vacation days, and growth opportunities to travel, bonuses, and even awesome office perks—free food, anyone?

The younger you are in your career, the more I'd encourage you to consider career growth opportunities over money. Early on, choosing the place that is going to teach you the most will give you the opportunity to learn valuable skills, making you more valuable in the future.

Negotiate Potential Outcomes

- **The counteroffer:** Once you've received an initial offer, you have some serious negotiating power. They want you, and they'd rather get to a number you're happy with than start the search all over.
  - Feel free to counter for more money if they've come in lower than your original salary requirement. If they have no flexibility in cash resources, appeal for more vacation days, a signing bonus, more equity, or even a greater annual bonus.
  - Stay within reason—keep your counter proportionate to the initial offer. Remember back to when the recruiter asked where you wanted to be salary-wise? Your counter-offer should fall within the ballpark range of their offer, so no one wastes the other's time. Chances are you'll land somewhere in the middle.
- **The firm "no," and negotiate for these things instead:** It's heartbreaking to hear "no," but don't give up. Instead, try approaching the conversation in a new way by asking for nonmoney perks. Some ideas include:

1. Monthly feedback
2. Stipend for career coaching or professional mentoring
3. Additional vacation time and/or sabbatical
4. Education or career development perks
5. Additional health benefits
6. Lifestyle perks
7. Performance bonus
8. Mental health/personal days
9. Work-from-home days and/or flexible schedule

- **The "I'll prove myself" bet:** You know what your work value is, but the best-fit-for-you company has never seen you in action. Sometimes this can lead to a "salary gap" that creates a negotiation impasse. You don't want to walk away, but you also don't want to accept less than what you deserve. One suggestion to resolve this gap is to accept the company's lower offer with an agreement for a set raise (to your preferred number) after you've shown what you're capable of doing—usually within three to six months. The fact is, companies hate to lose good employees. Investing in yourself to become "that" employee is a definite Power Move.

You've heard it before: the most successful negotiations are those in which both parties feel as though they've "won." That's a bit misleading. I prefer to approach a salary negotiation not as a contest where one party wins but as an exercise in which both parties are seeking to find fair value. Thinking this way relieves a lot of anxiety because you are both seeking the same thing and you'll be prepared to show that your value is completely justified. That's a major Power Move!

Final Thoughts

I wrote *Power Moves* because I am genuinely excited about what I've learned. Six years ago, I started Career Contessa, and ever since I've had this incredible opportunity to interact with thousands of women—to hear their stories, challenges, advice, and goals. There was never a question of what they wanted, but we all struggle from time to time on how to get it. Their lessons pulled on every emotion I have, but what I felt the most was a sense of pride. We are strong. We are resilient. We want careers with purpose and meaning, and, yeah, sometimes we need a little guidance.

My personal evolution uncovered the Power Moves approach. It was a career changer, nothing short of transformational for me. Starting slowly and building momentum, Power Moves have enabled me to see things with a clarity that I might never have had. They have helped me craft solutions for difficult business challenges; they've helped me use failure as fuel, and to calm my inner critic; they've given me confidence to do the unplanned thing. Most of all, making Power Moves has taught me to see that success is a work-in-progress practice—something that I look forward to courageously participating in each day.

You're here because you want more. Whether you're just starting, ascending the ladder, pivoting, or rebooting, I can confidently say that you are more than ready to start developing your own Power Moves approach. With that thought, I'm going to share (and even repeat!) a few final takeaways that might help you push ahead when the challenge seems to be too much, when support is nowhere to be found and your inner critic is winning the debate.

This really is something you can do, and I will be one of your biggest fans.

Power of Progress

When I was a freshman in college, I skipped the Freshman Fifteen and gained about thirty pounds. By the time summer rolled around, I was really motivated to lose some of the extra weight and started Weight Watchers. It was hard work, but I did get myself to a healthier weight in a healthy way. That experience also helped me adopt a valuable habit that I now apply every day—progress, not perfection.

The basic concept of my diet experience was to focus on portion control versus eliminating entire foods—with the belief that small changes would add up to a healthy and sustainable weight loss. This same thinking can be used to manage your career. Taking small steps each day that add up to something bigger is far easier, more sustainable, and ultimately more successful than any quick fix. It's also important to keep it real. Setting overambitious goals that are not met can negatively impact your ability to make progress. All or nothing might be a great strategy for jumping into the pool, but it doesn't translate well to real life.

So start small, maintain your momentum, and reap steady rewards. The fact is, continued progress of any type is the most effective way to create a sustainable long-term change.

Take It Easy on Yourself

Speaking with a lot of personal experience on the subject, one of the biggest, easiest to identify, and sometimes most confounding impediments in your career is you! Let's face it, all this stuff about ambition, expectations, dreams, perfection, and not quitting can be a real challenge. How can you possibly be content under the endless pressure you put on yourself that also easily distracts you from enjoying the journey? So take a step back and learn to appreciate who you are, what you've accomplished, and what you bring to the party.

I know, easier said than done. I'm not suggesting that you give up on your goals or that you give yourself a pass to quit. Quite the contrary: keep it going but recognize that you need to encourage yourself, not create a wall. Stop comparing—unless you want to acknowledge your gratitude—and focus on the steps that you can take each day to get the career you want, on your terms. Recognize not all progress is forward, but as long as you keep moving, as long as you keep making Power Moves, you'll be okay. In fact, better than okay.

Embrace Change

It's fair to say, you can count on change. If there's any question of this, just look around. Smartphones, electric cars, online education, rented resources—the list is endless. Big companies fail; start-ups lead. The speed of life and work is faster than ever, and there is no reason to think this "trend" won't continue. The way we deal with change is important for two reasons.

First, change can be really uncomfortable. Particularly when it comes to careers. The unexpected can be challenging, but when we accept change as inevitable and adopt Power Moves as an approach to managing our careers, we establish a pattern of initiating change for ourselves. We become familiar with the power of progress, and change is easier to handle.

Second, with change comes opportunities. I have no idea what my career, or work in general, will look like in five, ten, or twenty years. But I'm pretty confident that whatever happens, there will be lots of new opportunities. My takeaway? Using Power Moves to manage your career will be more valuable than ever. And developing a mind-set that helps you see the opportunities as they present themselves, instead of only the risks, will allow you to control your career.

Tune Out the Noise

There are times when you're going to feel completely lost in your career; all of us experience this. And during these times you may feel small or scared and like you have no idea what to do next. You'll have setbacks of your own making, do things like burn up a few years working a job you don't love around people you don't like in a career that is not for you. On top of this, the world is going to throw curveballs your way: layoffs, inequities, discrimination, times when it all just seems wrong. It's going to tell you no again and again—that you're not the right fit, that "they're going in another direction," that this dream cannot be yours. But here is the beauty of Power Moves: you have a way to handle it all.

Now, no matter what, you're in control of your career. You're ready to follow your own path and listen to your own voice. It won't always be easy. Roadblocks will continue to appear, but those sounds you hear are just distracting noise. Focus on what you really want—and start taking small steps to get it. If some fail, don't despair. You know you'll become better because if it.

Wherever you are in your career, whatever challenges you're facing, try one small Power Move each day—don't pressure yourself to do more or even require "success." A Power Move that lasts thirty seconds is still progress!

It's a Lifestyle

What I hope you'll do now, after reading this book, is start today, this minute, making decisions that are right for you, not just "right." Your career awareness has already expanded. Use it to harness your own power, take control of your career, and propel you into a working life that you want, that works for you, in the right here and the right now.

Building a career full of Power Moves—developing your own Power Moves approach—will always be and should always be a work in progress. It's an approach that becomes a lifestyle. It builds upon itself. It's something any of us can do to experience the career we want, on our terms. The only way to not make progress is to not move at all. *Take your power back.*

And that's the greatest Power Move of all.

The 14-Day Career Detox Power Move

We would like to take this time to insert micro-Power Moves throughout your entire workday, one element at a time. Take the next 14 days to challenge yourself to disrupt your day in different ways. Whether it's changing up your commute to work, taking lunch with coworkers you haven't gotten to know, or limiting your social media screen time, these are all habits that can feed into big change.

Here are just a few ideas to start making small (but meaningful) power moves throughout your work day.

MAKING POWER MOVES IN YOUR MORNING ROUTINE

- Don't press snooze
- Keep your alarm clock far from your bedside table
- Eat breakfast
- EXTRA CHALLENGE: Make yourself a delicious breakfast
- Make coffee at home (if you usually buy it)
- Have tea instead of coffee
- Exercise
- Go for a walk
- Hang out with your dog or cat
- Read a book (before you look at your phone)

- Don't look at emails until you get to work
- EXTRA CHALLENGE: Don't look at your phone until work
- Get to work early
- EXTRA CHALLENGE: Be the first person to the office
- Bring your coworkers doughnuts (I am secretly hoping someone at Career Contessa will accept this challenge)
- Have everything ready the night before (clothes, keys, lunch, etc.)
- Pack a lunch
- Call your Mom (or your Dad, or your sister)

MAKING POWER MOVES IN YOUR COMMUTE

- Listen to a new audiobook or podcast
- Take a different route
- Leave before traffic (if possible)
- EXTRA CHALLENGE: Walk or bike to work
- Call Mom (or Dad, or sister) from the car

- Carpool with a coworker or neighbor
- Get a ride to work
- Avoid listening to the news
- Sing in your car
- Get off the train a stop early and walk
- Go to the gym directly from work

MAKING POWER MOVES AT LUNCH

- Go out to eat with a new coworker
- Take your lunch outside
- Go for a walk
- Eat something new
- Try a new restaurant in the neighborhood

- Start a weekly team lunch
- Start a gratitude journal
- EXTRA CHALLENGE: Get lunch with your entire team (including your boss)
- Read for 30 minutes during lunch

MAKE POWER MOVES DURING MEETINGS

- Bring a new idea to a meeting
- Add your input
- Ask one question
- EXTRA CHALLENGE: Create a stunning visual presentation
- Create your own agenda for typically uneventful weekly meetings
- Take a meeting to discuss something with your boss
- Talk to your boss about meetings that seem unnecessary
- Create new meetings for your department to gain clarity on projects

MAKING POWER MOVES WITH YOUR COMMUNICATION HABITS

- Forget Slack and talk to a coworker
- Keep your personal phone out of sight
- Try getting rid of filler words like "just" or "sorry" in emails
- Check email only during allotted times (ie. 9-10 a.m, 3-4 p.m.)
- Make dedicated time to check in on all correspondence
- EXTRA CHALLENGE: Proofread everything you write (even on Slack) before sending
- Mind your emoji usage :)

SMASH DISTRACTIONS WITH THESE POWER MOVES

- Log out of all social media for one hour
- Log out of all social media for one day
- EXTRA CHALLENGE: Log out of all social media for an entire week
- Put headphones on to limit outside interruptions
- Ignore your work wife for an hour (she will understand)
- Install a productivity-based Chrome extension
- Close out your 30+ open tabs
- Create an away message on Slack or Google Chat (and use it)

POWER UP THE 3 O'CLOCK SLUMP WITH THESE POWER MOVES

- Delete all spam emails
- Unsubscribe from promotional emails
- Make a to-do list for tomorrow
- Clean your laptop screen (hello, fingerprints)
- Listen to a new podcast
- Take an online class to refresh your skills
- Join a live webinar
- Go for a quick walk
- Update your email signature
- Make a list of hobbies you'd like to learn
- EXTRA CHALLENGE: Start a women's committee at work
- Tackle our list of things to do when you're bored at work

REINVIGORATE TIME MANAGEMENT WITH THESE POWER MOVES

- Say no to happy hour
- Say no to unnecessary meetings
- Delegate some of your work
- Front load your morning with work
- EXTRA CHALLENGE: Do your least favorite + most cumbersome task first
- Create some to-do lists
- Prepare the next steps for all to-dos

Acknowledgments

My mother and sister for their sound advice and endless support.

My husband for being on my "team."

My agent for making this book a reality and circling back a year later to make sure I wrote a book proposal.

My publisher and editor for believing in me, talking me off the ledge many times, and helping me make *Power Moves* a reality.

The women interviewed in this book—thank you for your time and vulnerability to share your stories to help all working women.

My Career Contessa coworkers—past and present—and contributors for their dedication, passion, and commitment to the Career Contessa mission.

My friends who have been my proofreaders, advice-givers, and cheerleaders. The calls, emails, text messages, in-person chats, Instagram DMs, preorders . . . they mean everything to me.

To my network of incredible female founders, authors, and professionals—thank you for your help to spread the message of *Power Moves*. Your support does not go unnoticed or unappreciated.

And finally, to all the lifelong Power Movers, doers, and learners. This book is for you.

Index

About the Author

LAUREN McGOODWIN founded Career Contessa in 2013. Previously, she was a university recruiter for Hulu, focused on hiring, employer branding, and program management. Lauren has a bachelor's in education from the University of Oregon and a master's in communication management from the University of Southern California, where she wrote her thesis on millennials and career resources. She lives in Redondo Beach, California.